NATALIE
ON THE STREET

BY ANN NIETZKE

NATALIE
ON THE STREET

BY ANN NIETZKE

CALYX BOOKS | CORVALLIS, OREGON

The publication of this book was supported with grants from the National Endowment for the Arts, the Lannan Foundation, and the Oregon Arts Commission.

Cover art by Claudia Cave.
Cover and book design by Cheryl McLean.

CALYX Books are distributed to the trade through Consortium Book Sales and Distribution, Inc., St. Paul, MN 1-800-283-3572.

CALYX Books are also available through major library distributors, jobbers, and most small press distributors including: Airlift, Bookpeople, Inland Book Co., Pacific Pipeline, and Small Press Distribution. For personal orders or other information write: CALYX Books, PO Box B, Corvallis, OR 97339, (503) 753-9384, FAX (503) 753-0515.

⧀∞⧁
The paper in this book meets the guidelines for permanence and durability of the Committee on Production Guidelines for Book Longevity of the Council on Library Resources and the minimum requirements of the American National Standard for the Permanence of Paper for Printed Library Materials Z38.48-1984.

Library of Congress Cataloging-in-Publication Data

Nietzke, Ann, 1945-
    Natalie on the street / by Ann Nietzke
        p.   cm.
    ISBN 0-934971-42-0 (alk.paper) : $24.95. — ISBN 0-934971-41-2 (pbk.) :
$14.95.
    1. Homeless women — California — Los Angeles. I. Title.
HV4506.C2N54   1994
363.5'082 — dc20   94-19652
                                                       CIP

Printed in the U.S.A.
9 8 7 6 5 4 3 2 1

In memory of my mother

Lottie Bell Joyner Tidwell
1903-1962

ACKNOWLEDGMENTS

ALL NAMES, DATES, specific locations, and other factual means of identification have been changed in order to protect individual privacy, most especially that of "Natalie" herself. In several instances, composite "characters" have been drawn from two or more actual persons for the sake of narrative convenience as well as in the interest of privacy. Any apparent similarities to factually existent people, agencies, institutions, or circumstances must therefore be considered coincidental.

Portions of this work were completed during a period of support from the National Endowment for the Arts, for which the author is deeply grateful. Special thanks to Jean Samuel and Nikki Smith.

An excerpt of this work appeared in *Calyx: A Journal of Art and Literature by Women,* Vol. 14:1, Summer 1992, and has been reprinted in the *Los Angeles Reader* (Vol. 15:18, February 12, 1993) and in *The Sun: A Magazine of Ideas* (August 1993). "Home Free: Natalie on the Street" appeared in *Icarus* 14 (Spring 1994).

Grateful acknowledgment is made to the following for permission to reprint: DEACON BLUES, Words and Music by DONALD FAGEN, WALTER BECKER © 1977 by the MCA Music Pub., A Div. of MCA, INC. All rights owned or administered by MCA PUBLISHING, A DIVISION OF MCA, INC. All rights reserved. Used by permission. Joan Didion's "On Morality" appears in SLOUCHING TOWARDS BETHLEHEM, © 1965,1968. Quoted by permission of Farrar, Straus & Giroux Inc., New York.

CONTENTS

PREFACE

THIS IS A PERSONAL ACCOUNT of my relationship with an elderly schizophrenic "bag lady" who lived one recent autumn on the streets of my central Los Angeles neighborhood. I call her Natalie here, though that was not her name.

From incidental references, I guessed that she had been in Los Angeles for many years, having lived variously on the streets, in hotels downtown, and in board-and-care or nursing homes. I was able to verify only her name and birthdate with any certainty, along with the fact that she had spent one month as a psychiatric inpatient at a local county hospital a year or so prior to our meeting. Natalie would have been in her mid-forties when deinstitutionalization began and may well have been among the patients released from state mental hospitals in the late fifties or early sixties.

What follows is neither a complete and narrowly focused "case study," in any traditional sense, nor a broad examination of homelessness and mental illness and America's complicated failures in compassion. What follows can perhaps be viewed as a glimpse at one contemporary American "lifeway" or, most simply, as the story of an unusual friendship.

Ann Nietzke
Los Angeles, California

HOME FREE: NATALIE ON THE STREET

I I THERE IS NO SIMPLE WAY, no easy or uncomplicated way, to look into the face of a filthy old woman on the street. We are frightened or saddened or repelled, feel guilty if not resentful, and then we avert our eyes. In a society that disdains old women even in the best of circumstances, we are naturally overwhelmed by those who belong to no person or place, those who in the very state of their existence violate every conventional notion of "femininity" and force us to remember death. If the old gal is crazy as well—and it seems so many of them are—we're likely to hurry past, cross the street, avoid her altogether.

When Natalie first appeared in my neighborhood with her shopping cart and her miscellany of plastic bags, she drew particular attention, not because "bag ladies" are an uncommon sight in central Los Angeles, but because she chose to navigate the sidewalks of our narrow residential streets rather than sticking to Vermont or Western Avenue, Santa Monica or Olympic Boulevard. Jogging past her on my daily morning route, I would take to the gutter, relinquishing the entire walkway to Natalie as she inched her cart along. If she looked my way at all it was with

anger and suspicion, but I greeted her consistently with a neighborly "Good morning."

"HAH!" she called back to me one day, her arm shooting
straight up and out to wave me on with vengeance.

Having spent much of my adolescence in small-town Mississippi, I am often still impelled to "say hey" to strangers: at 7 a.m.
I will greet any female I meet and any male who lacks an overtly
menacing aura. There is no doubt, too, that my part-time cleri-
cal job in a psychiatric shelter for homeless people has deepened
my tolerance for unusual behavior and broadened my perspective on who looks or does not look threatening. So I would always call out "Good morning" to Natalie, until occasionally she
would give me a stiff, childlike wave (from the elbow down), not
smiling, demanding loudly of the space between us, "What's *her*
hurry-hurry-hurry?"

Even my lazy pace must have seemed rapid to her, pushing a
resistant cart stuffed with clothing and bedding, piled high with
paper and plastic bags themselves overloaded with who knew
what. She would shove the cart a few feet and then have to re-
trace her steps for the four or five auxiliary bags behind her, set
them carefully down again and give the cart another push.
Progress was slow, without apparent destination, and the tech-
nique, which seemed to require her full concentration, was obviously tedious and exhausting. As the weeks went by I noticed
Natalie standing wearily for longer and longer periods between
locomotions, though she would keep her hands on the red
handlebar of the cart as if at any second she might move on.

"That's what that officer told me," she whispered to me later
on. "Keep moving, see. As soon as I quit moving is right when
the trouble starts."

For most Americans the word *homeless* has become common enough to have lost both its shock value and its power to stir us. It is one of those adjectives that has crossed over to categorical noun: the blind, the deaf, the mentally ill, the disabled, the poor, the elderly, the homeless. But to endure homelessness for any extended period of time and still maintain integrity of the self requires more "sanity" than many of us possess; those who are less tightly wrapped to begin with can be easily undone by the streets. To lack a home is to lack, most basically, shelter from the elements. But that lack of shelter also means no toilet facilities, no place to cook food, no place to bathe or wash hair or change clothes, no place to store belongings. We say *home* is where we *live*, as if we cannot live without one. "At home" we can be at ease and comfortable ("Make yourself at home"). Our *residence* is where we *reside* (from the Latin "to sit back" or "remain sitting"). Having an *abode* is what enables us to *abide*—to bear the difficulties and sufferings of life, to tolerate and endure and restore ourselves to the world. Lacking a home we lack protection from the wickedness of strangers, we lack the dignity of belonging somewhere, we lack the privilege of determining who is welcome to be near us and who is not. We lack, finally, the identity that comes with having an address, which in some deep way serves to register formally our presence on earth.

For Natalie no dwelling place meant no place to "stay," implying her constant mobility. While for most of us "moving" means changing abodes, for Natalie it just meant keeping out of everyone's way. Her shopping cart functioned simultaneously as luggage, van, closet, cabinet, and furniture in what had become her traveling *apartment*, which she used to set herself *apart* from her environment on the street, where her personal boundaries came to include not just her person but her cart and bags as well. One could never deal with Natalie alone; one had to deal with Natalie and the cart and *all* her bags, whose number varied daily, mostly upward. Despite a lifetime of debilitating schizophrenic illness, Natalie's perceived need for a home and her ability to improvise one for herself represented to me a core of sanity within her that refused to budge. Though the cart was full of clothing she never wore and bedding she never used, and the bags held mostly waste paper, rotting food, garbage, and feces, these possessions enabled Natalie to claim her space as her own wherever she went and thereby maintain a sense of dignity and pride (telling me more than once that she knew people were jealous of her things, which sometimes caused her to feel sorry for them).

"What have you been doing today, honey?" she asked me one day after we became friends.

"Not much," I said. "Mostly just cleaning my apartment."

"This place needs straightening, too," Natalie said, in perfectly normal woman-talk. "I need to reorganize everything." She surveyed her belongings, grouped along the sidewalk near her cart, with the critical eye of any decent housekeeper. "I need some more bags, is what I need. But I just don't seem to have the time. Every day around here is busier than the last one."

I suppose if Natalie had been able to keep on the move as instructed, I might never have gotten involved with her. But looking out my window early one October morning, I realized that she was still lying flat on the sidewalk alongside her cart, that in fact it had been several days since I'd noticed her sitting up, much less standing in her usual manner. Dread gathered in the pit of my stomach, dread that she might be injured or sick or even dead, and that I was going to be the one to find out which it was.

"She's moved," I told myself. "She's probably moved a dozen times and ended up back here to sleep." But on my way out to work I knocked for my next-door neighbor. "Have you seen that woman across the street up and around the past few days?"

"Who?" Joyce said. "The bag lady? I think she's been over there all week long."

Crossing kitty-corner I braced myself. This approach felt very different from running past her incidentally. If she were sick she might not appreciate being disturbed. A madwoman, after all, is often an angry woman—I had more than once heard Natalie loudly scolding real or invisible passersby. I stopped in the street eight or ten feet from where she lay covered head-to-toe with what looked like a black garbage bag over a dirty, thin, white cotton sheet. The strip of grass between her and the curb still held its share of dew, but maybe the plastic had kept her dry.

"Lady?" I called out. "Excuse me, lady. Hey, lady?"

She sat straight up with an almost violent suddenness, apparently startled from sleep. She gazed at me with a kind of blank and groggy sweetness instead of the usual suspicion.

"I'm sorry," I said. "Are you all right? I just wanted to check and see if you were all right. Are you all right? Are you sick?"

"No," Natalie said softly. "I just haven't combed my hair yet. They tell me to comb that hair in the morning. You know." Her pale, blondish-gray hair, not quite shoulder length but getting there, hung straight from beneath the tight, light blue knit cap she always wore. What looked like a wig in a small paper bag she kept handy in her cart turned out to be her own hair, salvaged from these vigorous daily combings.

"So you're not sick, then," I said. "I hadn't seen you move for so long I was afraid something was wrong."

"Resting," she said. "I have to rest for the weary, don't I? They don't want me to wear myself down."

"So you can still walk all right?"

"Sure," she whispered confidentially. "This one and that one and the other one. You know."

"Well, do you have food and water? Do you have everything you need?" Natalie ignored the stupidity of this question and said, "Oh, yes," with conviction.

"Everything I need is here. Except I have to find that comb."

I figured Natalie to be in her late sixties, and then, when I thought of it, I subtracted a few years to compensate for the way her illness and life on the streets must have weathered her. It was shocking to learn later on that she was seventy-four years old, though as soon as I heard the number I realized that she looked every bit of seventy-four and more—in voice, in manner, and in the slow, cautious way she shuffled along when no one was pressuring her. Something in me had needed to keep her under seventy, as if that were the bitter, arbitrary age past which her homelessness became unbearable to contemplate.

Gradually I began to suspect that she must have recently been released from a hospital or nursing facility, if not a board-and-care home, and one day I glimpsed a plastic name band on her wrist, though I was unable to read what it said. "They tell me not to show that, honey," she whispered when I asked, and the next time I looked it was gone. Natalie's clothing appeared to have been chosen carefully with regard to both color and practicality for the street. She wore a very heavy, long wool skirt, dark blue with a diagonal stripe of burgundy, and her dark blue nylon carcoat, a zip-up model with several pockets, matched it perfectly. Only her shoes and stockings seemed insubstantial—plain black flats with nylons instead of something sturdy and warm with socks. The light blue knit hat complemented her eyes, and then there was the final touch—white nylon church gloves with all the fingertips cut off. The left fourth finger was slit vertically as well, just enough to reveal a plain silver ring containing a small, highly polished, dark blue marbled stone. The clothes were hardly fresh, but neither were they soiled and smelly. The skirt, though several clothespins were necessary to hold it up, was superior to pants because it kept her covered as she squatted to urinate and defecate. The jacket pockets, inside and out, held Natalie's most personal belongings (such as comb and makeup) and served in place of a purse. I kept wondering if Natalie had managed to set herself up so skillfully or whether someone had helped prepare her for life on the street (or *back* on the street), but questions designed to draw out her "story" only inspired bizarre combinations of memory and fantasy.

"Clark Gable, oh yes, he's a friend of mine. And of course Sammy Davis, Jr., was there, too. They tell me to let my hair grow longer now. That was on the corner down there on Third Street where they had that fireworks celebration. They keep track of it all in Sacramento."

"Well, are you a Californian, then?" I asked.

"He told me. I mean, I'm not supposed to say, but he said you can't help it, that's what you are, you're a CALIFORNIAN!!! Shhhh. There's no need for everybody to hear everything."

"Do you like to take a drink once in a while?" I asked, wondering if she might have just been through detox.

"Oh, no, no, honey," she whispered. "I don't even smoke a cigarette. I used to take a drink once in a while, but I have to be careful now." She looked around as if someone were eavesdropping. "You know."

"It's true," I said. "You do have to be careful out here. Do you ever hear voices speaking to you? You know what I mean? Voices?"

"No, I don't hear any voices, honey." She was answering very much in earnest, though what she said was plainly untrue. "I have had trouble with people disappearing, though. I'll look up and they'll be gone. Just like that. Boy-o-boy-o-boy. What would you make of that?"

"Aren't you afraid out here?" I asked her. "Won't you let me take you to a shelter where you can at least sleep indoors at night?"

"I'm better off in the open air," she insisted. "They gave me lye in there, you know. Put it all the way down my throat." She rubbed her throat as if it were sore.

"Well, aren't you afraid after dark out here?"

"I'm not afraid of the dark. Are you afraid of the dark, honey? So many people are, I know. I used to get those shots for nine dollars. Then they gave me the lye. And I used to be able to wash at that faucet behind the drugstore. Over here on Vermont. But the emperor tells me not to wash too much now, anyway. It's the Negroes, honey. They're trying to stay young at our expense. Believe me. But as far as a Californian, they've got all the necessary information in Sacramento, so it doesn't matter wherever I go or not. This and that and the other thing. You know." She winked her conspiratorial wink.

"Yeah," I said. "I know."

When I returned home the day I first checked on Natalie, she had managed to relocate her cart and bags about thirty or forty feet west of the corner where she'd been camping all that week. She may have taken my approach as a subtle hint to move on rather than as genuine concern, but whatever the motivation, it was extremely fortunate, since she would probably not have survived the night in her previous spot. Not long after midnight I was awakened by a thunderous crash, accompanied by a loud rush of water. A car had apparently run the stop sign beneath my window, then jumped the opposite curb, tearing a fire hydrant from its moorings and crashing into a palm tree before coming to rest on the very section of sidewalk where Natalie had lain for so long. No one in the car seemed to be hurt, but the pavement was soon flooded, water gushing down the gentle incline in front of my apartment building with all the resonance of a mountain creek. Two police cars, a firetruck, a water department van—all arrived in turn with flashing lights. Whenever incidental headlights approached the corner, I could see Natalie up the street, standing at the ready behind her cart, facing away from all the commotion, conspicuously minding her own business.

No arrest was made, though I found it hard to believe a sober driver could have accomplished such an accident. Eventually the police and fire department pulled away, leaving the Water and Power man to maneuver beneath the car with his various tools until he found the magic connection that subdued the flow to a trickle. Then the three young men from the car spent several minutes assaying damage. There was some discussion of whether they'd be able to back up over the hydrant without making things worse, but finally, with much grinding and scraping, they did get the car off the curb and into the intersection, where the motor died and refused to revive, oblivious to their curses in both Spanish and English. They pushed the car on down the street then and left it parked alongside Natalie, who scurried out of their headlight range and hid behind her cart as the boys walked off into the damp autumn night.

Coming back from my run late the next morning, I stopped to say hello to Natalie, who was up and alert, sitting on the sidewalk behind her cart with a blanket over her legs.

"A lot of excitement last night, huh?" I said. "I'm so glad you moved away from that corner."

"They say it's best to keep moving." She spoke with a tone of pride in having done the right thing.

"No, I mean I think that car might have hit you if you'd stayed where you were," I said.

"You never know what they'll do," she said firmly, not whispering. "They'll beat you to a bloody pulp."

"I mean the car that hit the fire hydrant," I said. "Did you hear all that water?"

"An uncle of mine was a fireman. Get all these babies and throw them down, you know? To save them? Burn 'em to a crisp if you didn't."

Obviously I was much more impressed by her brush with death than Natalie herself, whose world seemed such a relentlessly dangerous place that she could take a great deal in stride.

"How about a cup of coffee?" I said. "Can I bring you a cup of coffee?"

Natalie reached quickly down into her nearest bag and pulled out the broken-off head of a hammer. "This is what I used to pry open that closet when I was nine years old," she said, holding it out for me to inspect. I didn't want to ask about the closet, real or delusional.

"I'm going to have some coffee," I said. "Can I bring you some?"

"Can't you give a man a little pleasure? Can't you give a man a little pleasure? That's all he would ever say." She sat silent for a moment, then looked at me direct. "I believe you've got some gray in your hair."

"Yes, I do," I said. "My hair started getting gray when I was twenty-eight years old."

"Well, mine started getting gray when I was nine years old." She laughed to let me know this was a joke, so I laughed with her.

"Have you got a cup I can use?" I asked. "I don't have any throwaway cups."

"They'll give you one," Natalie said. "Go over here to the do-nut house."

"No," I said. "I'm bringing it from home. From where I live. Do you like cream and sugar?"

"Don't put anything in it to make me sleep. I don't have any trouble sleeping."

"You want cream?" I asked again.

"Not if it's gonna put me to sleep. I don't know why, but they always put something in it to knock me out."

"I'm not going to do that," I said. "I would never do that. I'm going to put some lowfat milk in it and some sugar. That's all. Do you have a cup I can use?"

Natalie began reaching for various plastic bags and rustling through their contents with some thoroughness. To me they all appeared the same, most filled with more plastic or with paper plates and trash and wads of paper, others stuffed with ratty-looking bits of cloth. Eventually she pulled out a sixteen-ounce styrofoam cup from Winchell's Donuts, reasonably clean with its lid still attached. She started to hand it to me, then jerked it back and removed the lid to peer inside. "Well," she said, holding it out for me to look. "That's what came out of me." Inside were two long, dark, solid, well-formed turds. "I hate to have to show that to you, honey," she whispered solemnly. "But there it is."

"There it is," I said. "I hate you had to, too." The urge to laugh was overcoming my disgust. "I'll just bring you a cup of mine and get it back later. Please. Don't search anymore." Natalie shrugged her shoulders and replaced the lid on the cup, which she then stuck back deep into its bag.

As I approached a few minutes later with the coffee, Natalie was on her feet, leaning against the cart and holding her side as if in pain. At the curb ahead of her the boys from last night had returned to work on their car. Natalie was grumbling to herself, and it soon became apparent that there had been a less than friendly exchange. I heard her mutter something about "sons-abitches," and the oldest boy, the driver, stepped from behind the raised hood to point at Natalie with pliers.

"If you don't like it here, go somewhere else," he said. "Nobody says you have to stand beside us. Take your garbage and go. Bag lady."

"Yeah," his younger and smaller companion chimed in. "Old bag lady. Why don't you go somewhere else? Old bag." All three of them laughed in the loud and easy way some Latino men seem to cultivate for outdoors.

I stopped in my tracks and stood glaring at them until they shut up and resumed business with their car. They had fallen from my good graces when they crashed into my sleep, and now I could feel blood pounding in my neck because I wasn't telling them off on Natalie's behalf as well as my own.

"They'll tear up everything you've got," she warned me as she sipped, ignoring my question about why she was clutching the side of her abdomen. "Watch your back every minute, I mean it. Somebody like you can't imagine the meanness that goes on in this world. What on earth did you put in there? It tastes awfully good."

"Milk and sugar," I said. "Coffee and water and sugar and milk."

It is perhaps remarkable that adolescent name-calling was the only overt and deliberate cruelty I witnessed toward Natalie during her whole time in the neighborhood. Eventually a number of women, in particular, went out of their way to be kind, partly no doubt from "motherly instinct" (it is always "women's work" to feed and clothe and cleanse the helpless). But in addition I think many women, especially unmarried women, have at least considered the fact that we live only a step or two or three from the streets ourselves and that in America the older we get the more precarious our positions become. With two words, *old bag*, a boy had reduced Natalie to an object of no more value than the thin sheets of plastic she used to organize and convey her life. Old bags. Old, dried-up breasts. Women past childbearing age, even proper, clean, sane ones, simply ain't worth what they used to be.

That autumn of the year Natalie appeared seemed cooler and windier and rainier than usual, though I may have just been more conscious of the nuances in weather because I was so keenly aware of her enduring it all unsheltered. For a time she parked her cart at the very far end of my block, directly on the corner where there was no tree to lean against, no shade, no structure of any kind to offer even minimal privacy or cover. I had to press my face sideways against my window screen to keep track of her there, and one afternoon when a chilly rain began to fall, I saw her kneeling completely unprotected beside the cart. By the time I dug up a thin blue plastic picnic cloth from the bottom of a drawer and got to her with it, someone else had already contributed a large sheet of sturdy, clear plastic, which Natalie was busy spreading over the cart and attendant bags rather than over herself.

"You better get under there," I told her. "It's raining harder all the time. Take this, too."

She took the tablecloth in both hands and stood with it folded tightly against her chest, as if I'd presented her a ceremonial flag.

"I wouldn't want to get this wet," she said. "It's so beautiful. Are you sure you don't need it?"

"Use it," I said. "Please. Put it over your head and shoulders before you get soaked." I was standing there with no umbrella myself.

"Oh, I'll dry out," Natalie reassured me. "He doesn't like me to be too dry, you know. And if you get him mad, then you've got trouble, so I'd about as soon not. You see what I'm saying."

"I see what you're saying," I said. "But let's just unfold the thing and put it around your shoulders, at least." I reached for the plastic.

NATALIE ON THE STREET |

"Well, if you want it back you can have it," she said, not, however, offering it. "You look like you're getting wet, honey. You've got the prettiest hands." We admired my hands for a while.

"I've got some gloves you can have," I told her. "Yours look a little breezy."

Natalie examined her protruding fingertips and laughed. "Oh, he likes me to wear these," she said pleasantly. "I don't know why." She spread the vertical tear on her ring finger to expose the bright blue polished stone for me.

"It's pretty," I said. "That's clever how you can show it off that way."

"Yes," Natalie said. "It's what you might call a basic heirloom, I guess. The whole arrangement."

"Have you had anything to eat today?" I asked her. I had brought her coffee several times but never food. Food felt like too much involvement, too much responsibility—that terrible commonsense admonition not to feed strays. "What have you had to eat today?"

"Nothing yet today," Natalie said. "I've got crackers a lady brought. Would you care for a cracker?" She began to rummage among the sheltered bags.

"No," I said quickly. "No thanks, I've eaten. What if I boiled you some eggs? Do you like boiled eggs?"

Her eyes lit up. "Oh, boy," she said. "I used to have them. I haven't had them anymore. But I don't want to run my bill up too high, you know."

"Don't worry about it," I said. "I'll be back."

I took her three hard-boiled eggs in a paper towel, along with a pink-and-gray knit hat and glove set, still in its gold display box from several Christmases ago. Natalie was lying flat on the sidewalk, head and all beneath the heavy clear plastic with her bags, still clutching the folded square of picnic cloth I'd brought.

"Eat them while they're warm," I told her. "They'll feel good in your tummy."

"Yes, I need to settle that stomach. I don't know what's the matter with it." She sat up on one elbow and took the eggs, though she was much more enthusiastic about the gold box than about the food or the new accessories. "You don't want to give that up," she said, quickly shoving it in amid her damp and airless, aromatic sacks. "It almost looks like the gift of the Magi, doesn't it?"

"Peel the eggs," I said, backing away. "Eat them now, before they get cold."

"Boy, they'll be good, too," she said, making no move. "Thank you ever so much."

"I can drive you to a shelter anytime," I said. "All you have to do is say the word."

"No, I'm already home free now, honey," she said. "Do I owe you anything for the eggs? They tell me not to run my bill way up."

Later that afternoon the rain slacked off, and I could see Natalie sitting up on her knees again, shaking out the blue plastic and then carefully refolding it to store away. She had replaced her light blue knit cap with the pink and gray one, which I took as a good sign, since the new one was thicker and warmer. Next morning, though, I noticed the blue cap was back—the hat-and glove ensemble, sans gold box, had taken its place among a wad of miscellaneous clothing in one corner of her cart and remained exactly there, I think, for as long as Natalie remained in the neighborhood.

Within a few days, something or someone caused her to break camp suddenly and move back to the corner directly opposite my building. She stood there poised with her cart in the mid-morning sun, shouting long enough and loud enough to penetrate through closed windows to the farthest side of my apartment, though except for scattered obscenities I couldn't make out her words. I boiled some eggs and went out to see what the fuss was about.

"YOU GET AWAY FROM HERE, BY GOD." I wasn't sure if she was talking to me because her eyes had a vacant, glazed look, and her head had not yet turned my way. I stopped in the middle of the street, though, ten or twelve feet away from her.

"Are you mad this morning, Natalie?" I asked. "I could hear you all the way upstairs. It sounds like you're angry at someone." She turned to face me and directed her full force of fury in my direction.

"YOU'D BE MAD, TOO, IF SOMEBODY PUT A BOMB IN YOUR CART AND TRIED TO BLOW YOUR FUCKING CART AWAY."

"Oh," I said, more calmly than I felt. Her cart didn't appear in the least disturbed since the last time I'd seen it.

"AND IF THEY TRIED TO TALK WHEN YOU DON'T FEEL LIKE HAVING A CONVERSATION." She stretched her neck and yelled this somewhere to the left and over my head, but I still felt it was aimed at me. I had a feeling neighbors were peeping out their windows to see what I was doing to make the shouting worse.

"So do you want some eggs?" I held them out for her to see.

"Yes, I do." She responded quietly in a rational tone of voice. I approached her quickly, handed them over, and retreated without hesitation.

"Thank you very much," she said, formal and polite.

"You're very welcome," I said. The storm, whatever it was, appeared to have subsided. Natalie arranged her bags at the base of the palm tree, spread out the furry black lining of an old coat on the sidewalk, and settled down for a stay of indefinite duration.

From that point on, by virtue of her proximity if nothing else, Natalie took up a unique kind of daily residence in my thoughts—I could no longer buy groceries, cook, discard leftovers, or deal with sacks, bags, or containers of any kind without some consideration of Natalie. Confronted each day with her tormenting lack of facilities, I would sit down on my toilet with conscious gratitude, climb into a warm bath with a heartfelt sense of luxury. During this particular period in my own life, circumstances allowed for a more than ordinary investment of energy in attending to Natalie: I was working a job three days a week but was otherwise reclusive, enduring a lengthy and painful separation in a long-term relationship and struggling to complete a novel under a self-imposed deadline. I was home a lot, and Natalie was "home" constantly, there on the street. By November I began to keep a journal that focused exclusively on her.

STRIKING HOME:
A DAYBOOK

Rain has continued for several days, and more is predicted. Natalie keeps her cart against the base of the palm tree, though the fronds afford her little protection. She has her thick sheet of clear plastic spread out to cover all her bags, and she makes her bed down the middle of this display, where she lies flat on the sidewalk, covered head to toe herself except between showers, when she folds back the plastic to breathe. She seems to lie down most of the time now, to the point where I am relieved whenever I see her standing up or moving around a bit. At least she doesn't have the swollen legs with ulcers that so many street women get when they stay on their feet too much or try to sleep sitting up.

Natalie is often sleeping when I approach and may be groggy but is not usually irritable at being awakened. I think she tries to stay alert and vigilant at night and lets herself doze during the day. She claims that the plastic keeps her dry enough, which I guess it does, but the lack of air underneath it is creating a thick, sour odor among her bags and clothing. The stench rises up and sometimes forces me back a step or two for air before I can give her the food I've brought. Her face and fingertips are blackened with grime now, and I hate to consider her hair, which is mostly tucked beneath the blue cap.

So far I have taken her eggs, soup, chicken and tomatoes, blackeyed peas and cornbread, pudding, crackers, V-8 juice, bananas and oranges, a bran muffin, and doughnuts. I have never actually seen her eat anything, but I can understand her wanting privacy. She is somewhat self-conscious about having no teeth, and sometimes she'll cover her mouth to smile or laugh. Thinking about feeding her reminds me I'm not so great at feeding myself in any regular, properly nutritious way. Cup-o-Noodles seems to suit us both. I hope to find some on sale this week and stock up.

"You look like Martha Washington today!" Natalie says. I think this is a response to my wearing a skirt instead of the usual sweatpants or jeans, but still I don't know what she means by it. There is no use asking, although I try.

"You know," she says. "Don't you know Martha Washington? I had almost given up on you today. I thought maybe you had to go to court."

"No, I was just a little late getting home from work," I say.

"Well, I knew you were in court. I didn't know when they'd let you out, if they ever would."

Sometimes when I approach I hear her talking softly, even pleasantly, to herself. "What's happening?" I'll ask.

"Oh, I'm reminiscing," she'll whisper. She is always asking me if I remember people or places or events—certain drunken men and pimps, certain hotels and streets, certain stabbings and explosions. She is sure I must have been there, that she knew me "back then," and she is always surprised anew when I say I don't remember. Today I hand her a plastic bag from Von's Market, and she mentions that it closed, which is true.

"Ann, you remember old Von's down there at First and Western. Don't you, Ann?"

"Yes!" I say. "Yes, I do! And you're right, it did close. Now it's a Korean store."

"Well, I'm glad you remember something," Natalie says, more exasperated than pleased, since this reminds her of how much I seem to have forgotten.

She is using my name a lot these days. Maybe she knows it pleases me.

| | NOVEMBER 6

Each day it's an ordeal to get Natalie to let me throw away some trash. It is difficult to get her to distinguish between her daily garbage and her permanent collection. Because she is staying in one place now, excrement is becoming a real concern, and I'm starting to approach her always with plastic bag in hand, in case she consents to let me carry the mess away.

Today she is sitting up between rain showers, keeping her legs stretched out beneath the plastic. I wonder how she can stand the hardness of concrete for such long periods, with only the furry coat lining between her and the dampness of the sidewalk. Beside her, on the grassy strip near the curb, is a bright pink box of thin cardboard, the kind birthday cakes come in. Maybe someone brought her leftover cake, but that's not what's in the box now—there is brown seepage around the bottom edges of pink. I coax her into lifting up the box and depositing it into the grocery bag I've brought, though she is reluctant for me to use a brand new plastic bag for this purpose. The stench is so bad I have to tie up the bag and carry it to the garbage bin behind my building before I can bear to stand and talk with her.

"What if I bring you some small plastic bags?" I say. "Some thick ones, like freezer bags. Do you think you could use them to go to the bathroom in? Number two, I mean?"

"No." This is a definite refusal, so definite I'm reluctant to pursue the subject, which feels intrusive anyway. I don't say anything for a while.

"I've got to learn to control these bowels, honey," she says then, and there is anguish in her voice.

"It's not as if you can control it," I say. "We just need a way to dispose of it."

"No, I can control it most of the time. But I don't get quite enough food, really, you know, and that makes it hard to do. And then if somebody's talking at you all the time about whether he's getting more food or you're getting more food, that can make you somewhat nervous. That doesn't help to control things either. See what I mean?"

"Maybe you can walk somewhere else to go," I say. "Find some hidden bushes or grass, so you don't mess up right where you're living here."

"You mean just walk away and leave everything?" Natalie looks at me as if this were possibly the most absurd idea she has ever heard in her life. She promptly agitates herself into a violent paranoid fantasy about what will happen if she takes her eyes off the cart—even for a moment. To hear her tell it, the neighborhood is brimming with people who not only covet her possessions but are just watching and waiting to see her destroyed, preferably blown to bits.

"INTO THIN AIR," she shouts. "CAN'T YOU UNDERSTAND ANYTHING?"

"So, Natalie," I say quietly. "Natalie."

"What?" Her tone descends to the usual pseudo-whisper.

"I have to go," I say. "What can I get you? Do you have any water?" This is always a complicated issue. Natalie often claims to have water, but I don't believe she does, and if she does, I don't think she drinks it.

"They don't understand how thirsty I get," she says. "I get so thirsty."

"I know why you get so thirsty," I tell her.

"Why is it?" she asks, genuinely curious to know.

"Because you don't drink enough water."

"Well, what goes in must come out, you know."

"I know," I say. "And what goes up must come down. What goes around comes around." We laugh. I know she avoids drinking water in order to avoid urinating.

She digs deep into one of the bags underneath her cart and pulls out a pint-size glass bottle that I gave her water in weeks ago. I am surprised she's remembered and kept track of it all this time, but she seems quite taken with the name "Socco," printed in black on the silver lid.

"Socco, Socco, Socco," she says gaily. "What on earth would you expect it to mean?" She studies my blank expression. "Soc-Soc-Socco. Just like a Socco. They all have their favorites, don't they?"

"So sock it to me," I say. "I'll fill it up for you."

"I don't know. Maybe so. Do you think so? Do you think it would work? I don't think so." She hugs the container with both hands, close to her heart. "He said not to give Ann that Socco bottle back," she whispers. "No telling. You say it's fine, but I'm the one he's gonna beat up. I hate to be hit like that, just beat to a pulp."

"Well," I say, "the hell with him." I have no idea how Natalie might respond to this. I feel as if I've taken a big risk, but she actually looks pleased, as if I've been a naughty, naughty girl but she is pleased with me anyway. "Just give me the bottle, and I'll bring you some water and the hell with him," I say again. "You'll have a nice fresh drink and he'll stay out of the way for a while."

Natalie lets out a mischievous, snorting laugh and hands over the jar, and when I bring it back, scrubbed clean and filled with cold water from the fridge, she unscrews the cap and drinks about half of it right away, one of the best things I've ever seen her do.

"There," she says, wiping her lips and chin on the back of her glove. "What about it?"

| | NOVEMBER 7

Finally a sunny day with no more rain predicted. Last week I asked Natalie if she would wash if I brought her a bucket of water and soap, and she said yes, she believed she would. I am hoping she (or "they" or "he") hasn't changed her mind. I decide to get Natalie her own bar of soap and think Ivory will be good since it will float in the bucket.

"Do you like Ivory?" I ask.

"Yes, Ivory's all right," Natalie says, not looking at me. There is a *but* here, slow in coming. "I prefer Caress," she says. "Really. Palmolive Gold is good. But Caress is the best. It makes your skin so soft."

I've never heard of "Caress," but the wizardry of American advertising reaches far and wide and deep—brand loyalty, even on the streets. After I get past my initial "beggars-can't-be-choosers" reaction, I have to laugh. Why can't beggars be choosers? Sure enough, the little Mexican market on the corner carries Caress, and when I bring Natalie the metal bucket full of warm water, she latches right onto the soap, very pleased and excited.

"Boy, I can use that. Can I use it? But how much was it? I can't run my bill way up. They tell me not to keep money, you know. They say not to show that money. I have to keep it...." Natalie rolls her eyes at me in such a way as to indicate that she must keep her money inside the front of her zipped-up coat. "They'll steal everything you let them. Hide it here, hide it there. You can't be careful enough, really. How much was it? If my bill gets too high, let me know. They don't like it when my bill gets way up."

"Seventy-nine cents," I say. "Let's not worry about it now." I'm afraid she's about to talk herself out of bathing after I've so consciously talked myself into it: I'm wearing old clothes and shoes and have vowed not to flinch.

When she is finally convinced that the soap is hers to use, that her bill is not too high, and that she doesn't have to pay me, which would involve showing me her secret money, Natalie consents to open the box of Caress and to accept the washcloth I've brought. It takes some coaxing to overcome her inhibitions about doing this cleansing in broad daylight. "He" and "they" seem to be lurking about, threatening and scolding and bossing her, which she tends to verbalize or respond to by muttering under her breath.

"Who do you think you are?" She keeps fussing with the box of soap. "Just who in the hell do you think you are, anyway?"

"Get up and let's do it," I say. "Let's do it right now. It'll make you feel good."

Natalie gets to her feet, and I am surprised at her strength when she suddenly lifts the bucket by herself. She missteps and is nearly pulled over but manages to set it right, close to the palm tree for privacy in that direction. I stand in front of her on the street side. Behind her, across a small yard, is a one-family house with no sign of activity, and on the other side the cart and bags lend at least the illusion of protection. Natalie takes her grimy gloves off, folds them neatly, and lays them on the sidewalk.

"They told me not to take these gloves off today," she says, testing me, I think, for reassurance.

"It doesn't matter," I say. "You have to take them off so you can wash. It's not going to be a problem."

She drops the washcloth into the bucket and then hesitates, unsure of what this procedure is going to involve.

"Step out of those shoes," I tell her, "and then give me your hose. I'm going to bring you another pair." Natalie is wearing black knee-high hose, which at this point are nothing more than several giant holes held together here and there by a strip of elastic and a strand of nylon. She looks at me as if I'm being naughty again, but complies anyway. Her toenails are a revolting sight, yellow and ill-formed and so long and thickened I don't think I own anything that could cut them. I open up a plastic bag and Natalie deposits the hose with an air of proud finality.

"Now the underpants," I say.

She chortles as if I've made some impossibly obscene request.

"What's funny?" I say. "Aren't you wearing any underpants?"

"What does *she* have in *her* mind?" Natalie turns to inquire this of the palm tree.

"Come on," I say, all business. "I'm going to bring you clean ones."

Natalie gives me a salacious wink and a silly, toothless grin as she bends over and, forsaking all modesty, hikes up her skirt and pulls down the panties, which are brownish-gray and soaked from the waistband down with what has to be fairly recent diarrhea. I manage to act as if I'm not giving this a second thought, hardly a thought at all, really, as they splat into the bag on top of the hose. I close the bag tight, double-knot it, and set it in the gutter several feet away, toward the corner. With her skirt still up in back, Natalie reaches for a stray piece of napkin that lies on the sidewalk beneath her cart.

"Excuse me," she says politely. "I have to wipe my a-hole," which she proceeds to do while I keep my back to her, grateful for the momentary absence of passing cars.

I get the Caress out of its box and hand it to her when she turns around. "Wash your hands in the bucket first," I tell her, and I wring out the washcloth while she accomplishes this. "Now your face. Do your face before anything else."

I stay long enough to make sure she's doing this before I hurry off to the garbage bin and then upstairs for clean things. I find some pale yellow knee-highs of sturdy texture and some pale green, stretchy cotton panties that I'm sure won't be too small. I wish I had a suitable skirt to replace the long woolen one Natalie has worn since her arrival. It is filthy now, as is her jacket, as is the jersey top beneath.

On my way out I knock for Joyce next door, to see if she might
have an old skirt—it needs to be long and warm and full enough
to allow for easy squatting. Joyce doesn't have such a thing but
pulls out a pile of sweatshirts and sweaters. I take a burgundy
sweatshirt with several pockets for Natalie and a navy blue hooded
and zippered one for myself to run in. I've been needing one but
haven't been able to find any for under fifteen or twenty dollars,
which seems exorbitant. Now I can wear Joyce's sweatshirt and
pretend I've saved twenty dollars, which theoretically gives me
leeway to buy quite a bit of food for Natalie before she "runs her
bill up too high."

When Natalie sees what I've brought, she declares, "You've
worked hard, and I've worked hard. I don't want you to do too
much. It's too much trouble. Isn't it?"

"I'm in the mood today," I say. "Catch me on the fly. Let's
do it."

"Well, OK then," Natalie says. She acts as if she's finished washing, and her face does look a lot better, though there are still
small areas of caked black dirt on one cheek. The water in the
bucket is murky brown, with bits of grass floating on top. Natalie
balances herself against the tree and sticks each foot in to soak
for a while.

"Feels so good," she says. "Dance with a dolly with a hole in
her stocking. Don't you think so, Ann?"

I hand her the old dishtowel I've brought for her to dry on,
and I leave both it and the washcloth in the bottom of the bucket
to throw away, once I've poured the water down the storm drain
at the corner.

"What did you say I owed you for the soap?" Natalie starts to
obsess again about the Caress, but she certainly confiscated it

while I was gone: it's nowhere in sight. I just hope she's keeping it in the box.

She is pleased by the bit of lace on the waistband of the panties. "My, my, my," she says, and pulls them up fast. Then leaning against her cart, she somehow manages to get the hose on standing up and, miraculously, avoids causing runs with those monstrous toenails. She slips into her black flats and walks around with a spring in her step, showing me how good she feels.

"You look great," I tell her. I think I feel happier than she does. Having achieved this much I wish I could get her really clean and into clean clothes, but she shows no interest even in the sweatshirt I've brought. She accepts it politely while rejecting the notion that she'll ever be able to change her clothes.

"They'll think I'm crazy," she whispers. "I have to be careful about wearing a man's clothes, honey." I reassure her that it's a woman's sweatshirt, but she's not buying this, I can tell.

"Promise me you'll at least try it on after dark," I say. "You need to have a clean shirt on now that you're so clean. We need to get rid of the one you're wearing. Promise?"

"Well, I promise," she says, straightening her furry bed on the sidewalk and settling down into her usual niche. "But nobody seems to get a certain point. He'll be up in my bowel before you can blink that eye, see. He doesn't like these gloves all over the ground like that."

I come home exhausted. Oddly it is not the odor of feces or stale sweat that clings to my clothing and hair but the smell of Natalie's collected stuff, a palpable odor from all those bags under the thick plastic cover for days in the rain. After a bath and shampoo, I carry my own clothes, knotted in plastic, down to the garbage bin, too.

| | NOVEMBER 8

This morning coming in from my run I see that Natalie did not change shirts during the night, and I make the mistake of mentioning this and expressing disappointment.

"WELL, I HAD COMPANY LAST NIGHT," she shouts—her defiant excuse for not doing as she promised. My disappointment has set her off. She keeps picking the burgundy sweatshirt off the top of her cart and then throwing it back again, pacing and muttering and justifying herself.

"They were out here bugging me the whole damn night," she says, angry but keeping the volume low. "They want to see everything, to start with, and then they'll grab it before you can turn the lock. They turn everything over and over and over again and leave you for dead, nothing but a bloody pulp. And then they expect you to take your clothes off right out on the street. MY GOD, ARE YOU OUT OF YOUR FUCKING MIND?"

I leave her abruptly, hoping she will settle down alone, but when I return later with coffee and corn muffins she is still upset—I can hear the resentful mumbling all the way across the street.

"Put this one on, put that one on." Natalie has laid out a very clean white knit sweater beside the burgundy sweatshirt. "This one, that one, this one, that one. I can't wear just anything at any time. If you take a man's clothes off, that's it. CAN'T YOU UNDERSTAND THAT? CAN'T YOU UNDERSTAND ANYTHING? SHUT UP AND GET AWAY FROM ME!"

She looks directly at me, though I haven't said a word. This shouting rage has a hollow ring to it, and after a moment or two I simply offer the food and drink, which she accepts and thanks me for. She sets both down on the sidewalk, at the inner edge of her furry mat, and she continues to pace and obsess about the sweatshirt, though references to this grow convoluted as she carries on and on.

"Listen, Natalie." I have to interrupt her to speak because it appears she could rush on forever. "Listen," I say. "It's really all right. You don't have to put the shirt on. Just do whatever makes you feel comfortable."

"How am I supposed to put the sweater on, too?" Natalie demands, as if I had tried to coerce her into both garments at once. "There she was, tugging on this arm till I thought she'd break it off. Whatever she wanted, I don't know. But they won't just let you wear anything in the world. Here he'll come with that big joint, trying to run it up my bowel." Suddenly she sits down, and I bend at the waist, hands on my knees, to tell her again that she doesn't have to wear anything new, that what she has on is fine.

"Don't bend over like that, honey," she whispers. "Anything could happen if you stand bent over that way. If you want to do it, you can do it, but if it was me, I wouldn't do it. He's got a big, black you-know-what, too. They're staying young at our expense."

I leave her to her breakfast and come home to mine, regretting yesterday's extraction of the promise. Underneath all the anger and defiance and confusion and craziness, I sense Natalie's anguish over not having pleased me. I mustn't make her promise anything again, because she probably won't be able to keep her word, which is apparently upsetting. I also think I need to be careful about telling her to do things—try to ask gently instead of tell. The voices in her head seem to give orders constantly, so that external suggestions must feel like interference, causing confusion and anxiety and intensifying the paranoia. I want to avoid saying anything negative or critical, too, if I can.

I'm sure one reason Natalie is afraid or reluctant to change shirts is that she has too many things stashed away inside the one she's wearing. Today I could see how bulky her upper chest appears inside the top of her half-zipped jacket. Probably she has her "papers" and I.D. and money there at least. I know she wears a bra that bothers her sometimes because I see her tugging at straps—quite possibly the cups are padded with possessions, too. I've seen her reach deep for lipstick—sometimes she will have a lot of bright blue eyeshadow on, with bright red lipstick smeared around her mouth, all very bizarre and caked with grime. She may be hypersensitive this morning because the bath—however good or necessary, well intentioned and even appreciated—was also a major intrusion of privacy.

| | NOVEMBER 9

Last night I didn't take food.

"Did you go to a premiere last night?" Natalie asks this morning.

"No," I say. "A poetry reading."

"Because I was really worried. A young fellow was hanging around here and hanging around after my things here. But the way you were all dressed up I figured you went to that premiere, you know."

"Just a poetry reading," I say again, but this appears not to register.

"So she came out and told him, YOU GET OUT OF HERE AND LEAVE THIS LITTLE GIRL ALONE. She told him I was raped in a field by my father's best friend when I was a little girl when he had a few too many. But she said DON'T YOU COME UP AND TRY TO GET UP BEHIND HER. NO WAY. Up behind in my bowel, you know. She told him good, too."

Natalie is alternately whispering and shouting. Nearby on the curbside grass is a small, sturdy plastic container covered with a pie tin that has lost its shine. Glossy green flies are swarming and buzzing furiously, trying to squeeze their way under the aluminum. There must be some natural logic here, this fierce attraction of flies to human excrement, but it's not a phenomenon I'm inclined to explore. The burgundy sweatshirt and the white sweater are still prominently displayed on top of Natalie's cart, laid out neatly as one might arrange tomorrow morning's clothes at bedtime.

"Do you want some eggs?" I ask.

"Yes," she says. "That would be nice, but not if you're busy doing other things. Then you mustn't bother."

"I have time," I say. "I work three days a week, but not today."

"Oh, you *work*." She seems surprised, though I've mentioned this before. "I didn't know you *worked*. So you *work*. You're a *worker*, then. You're a *working* girl. No wonder you look so tired. You better get some rest. All those jobs and the wear and tear and so on. It's too much for you, really, isn't it?"

Sometimes it is, as a matter of fact, and I don't mind getting a bit of sympathy once in a while, either.

I worry about feeding Natalie so many eggs, but they seem perfect for her—they don't require teeth and can be eaten warm or cold, now or later, and are protected from the filth by their shells. She seems to love them, and for me they're easy to fix, economical, and easy to clean up after. I return to her with eggs and crackers, armed with triple plastic bags.

"Oh, what are these little crackers?" Natalie sniffs at the food, first one nostril, then the other. "These eggs look so good, don't they? What kind of a cracker are these?"

"Wheat Thins," I tell her. "I think they're called Gourmet Wheat Thins."

"Oh, gourmet. Oh, my goodness. They would be delicious, then. Don't you think so? Do you ever eat them, Ann? You don't eat them, I bet. Or do you? Do you eat them yourself? Or not? You do? You like 'em? You do, huh? They must cost if they're gourmet. Don't run me up too high."

Natalie stashes the paper saucer and paper towels with eggs and crackers right behind the nearest wheel of her cart, and I pull plastic bags from beneath my shirt to begin the delicate negotiations over what she'll let me throw away today. We both watch the flies for a while, and I can tell by her sidelong glances that she doesn't want to disturb the mess.

"It's pea soup," she says finally. "Just leave it. She brought me all that greasy soup she made me eat." I unfold a double plastic bag. "You can have it if you want it," Natalie says. "I don't want it." She lifts up the pie pan, revealing dark brown liquid, and dumps it with the container into my wide open bag. I close it up tight with double knots and hold it at arm's length. Natalie surprises me then by picking out another bag of paper trash for me to take. In exchange I give her the

extra bag I've brought. She surveys her domain and looks perplexed.

"I need new bags," she says. "Look at this. Half of 'em worn
out after the rain. I need to take everything out and put it into a
new one." She gets agitated when she realizes I'm taking away
more bags than I've given her, even though they were mine to
start with. "I CAN'T GIVE UP TWO AND ONLY GET ONE BACK,"
she shouts as I back away, hoping to outdistance the flies, if not
the stench.

"I'll bring new bags when I can," I say, but Natalie is thoroughly displeased.

The trash barrels behind my building are nearly full, a welcome sign that means pick-up time is soon. I toss in Natalie's
featherweight bag and then gingerly lower the one with excrement. It looks secure enough, but after I come upstairs I start to
worry, so I go back down with a paper bag inside another plastic
one. Already the bin smells bad, and there are flies. The extra
sacks make a definite improvement, but I come back up still concerned and feeling guilty. I know my landlady, Mrs. Moller downstairs, would throw one of her famous conniptions if she knew. I
wash my hands in the bathroom sink, then again in the kitchen,
savoring the comfort of porcelain and warm running water.

| | NOVEMBER 10

It is hot today, sunny and clear and into the eighties. When I
take her bananas and juice, Natalie is sweating and says she has
a headache.

"Maybe getting out of the sun would help," I suggest, but she pays this no mind. In the bright, concentrated heat both Natalie and her bags are more odoriferous than usual.

"It could be a cold," she whispers. "I told you about them stealing that money, didn't I? After I won that $45,000 at the track and it's gone in a slap, just like that? So what can you do? All the babies I delivered were perfect. No club feet or anything, after I went into that field. They all wanted me to be the one to deliver them, you know. No one else will believe me, but maybe you will, Ann. The big guy was giving these boys, the tall ones I mean, he was giving them pills that made them kids again. I've seen it in the schoolyard. I try to hold that gas in when the kids are around. Then if they leave I'll let go, you know, and hope it's just gas."

She claims not to have any "trash" for me to take. I give her a new plastic bag anyway, but she is too disturbed and distracted to take much pleasure in it today. Her speech is even more pressured than usual, sometimes seeming improvised. When I squat beside her with my hands folded together, she incorporates me right into the fantasies. "And he said not to say anything to the one squatting down with her hands folded up. She came over here just looking like a corpse, and I said honey, you need to get some rest or something."

Natalie is sweating profusely but apparently does not consider taking off her jacket and knit hat and gloves. The gloves are in tatters now and filthy. I don't dare suggest she take anything off, since for her removing any item of clothing seems tantamount to disrobing altogether.

"Oh, yes, I went to a lady's house," she tells me. "She kept saying come over, come over, come over and take a shower. She got me in there and...you know. You know what I mean. I was out of there in a hurry, I can tell you that. *She thought I would take off all my clothes! She did!*" Natalie looks at me and laughs as if the woman were out of her mind.

"Really?" I say. "But how could you take a shower with your clothes on?"

"See what I mean?" Natalie says, insinuating with her voice that the woman's motives were sexual. "See what I mean? That's exactly what I told her, too."

Suddenly the winter ahead looms long and difficult. Natalie rambles on and on while I sit wondering how she can keep living this way.

"It's just a matter of concentrating," she says. "But sometimes I do hold it in till it hurts." She fiddles with the clothespins at the waistband of her skirt.

"Maybe you're sick," I say. "Maybe you need to see a doctor. Or maybe you could let me take you somewhere near a shelter. You could get some regular food. And maybe use the restroom there." This sets Natalie off, as it has in the past. I should have known better than to bring this subject up today.

"THAT'S WHAT THEY KEEP ASKING ME ALL THE TIME, ALL THE TIME. HE'S NOT GONNA ALLOW IT."

"You don't have to shout," I tell her. "Just talk to me, I can hear you fine."

"Well, that's what happened when I was down at the Strand Hotel." She returns to a whisper, but a very urgent one. "You know, down at Union and Seventh where Monroe was shot? I had this other place, but you had to have luggage to check in there. And he took a stick and just hit me as hard as he could across the neck and all across the shoulders." She uses both hands to point to the site of the beating. "My father fought with him. But this Clarice or whatever her name is comes over here and wants this and wants that. See, they put something into the coffee to wake me up. That's why I stopped going to coffee shops, like I told you a couple of days ago. They'll put something in there to speed you up, this Dexedrine. They put it in there so you'll get up and move away from there, see. Which is exactly what I mean."

| | |

This evening I take her a cup of beef bouillon. She once asked if I had any, so today at the store I got bouillon cubes along with a package of sixteen-ounce styrofoam cups—I've grown weary of trying to figure out what containers to use for her and bargaining to get them back. Natalie says she will like the bouillon as long as it doesn't make her thirsty, which leads into our typical exchange over water: whether she has any, whether she drinks any, whether a drink is worth the price she has to pay in urine. She seems to be in an unpleasant mood, not talkative for a change, and not receptive to much talk from me. This withdrawal causes me to realize how accessible Natalie is most of the time, in spite of everything. I do believe she is sick with a cold.

As I return home, two women are sitting on the front steps of my building, chatting in the dusky light. One is Velma, my downstairs neighbor, and the other is a petite, white-haired woman I've noticed around the neighborhood for years, always on foot and always wearing some sort of jaunty hat. Velma introduces her as May.

"You can do as you like," May tells me. "But you know, our senator's office sent a public health worker out here to see this woman." She gestures vaguely in Natalie's direction. "She offered to take her to a shelter and gave her a number to call and money to make the call and everything else. I guess it was raining, so this worker even offered to take her home with her that night and find out what benefits she's eligible for and everything else. And she told me if people feed the poor thing it's just encouraging her. If nobody feeds her she'll move on. I called them because she's living over there like a public health hazard. That's so much worse than an eyesore. Of course, you can do as you like."

"I will, thanks," I say.

Too much blood rushes to my head in these situations, and a throbbing sets in at the temples and base of my neck. When there is too much to be said, I feel defeated before I begin—too little tolerance and a failure of courage in the face of such cool, authoritative ignorance. In years past I would likely have come straight upstairs with a headache, but tonight I stay the course and get into a lengthy, convoluted discussion about mental illness and homelessness. May called the senator, after all, and not the police, though Velma would have preferred she call the police. Velma is a lively woman in her early fifties with a jet black, modified beehive hairdo and an "I ♥ ■ DANCING" bumper sticker on her car. Velma doesn't care much for Blacks, Hispanics, Asians, Jews, or anyone who doesn't work for a living, which includes Natalie. Both women seem shocked and bewildered when I try to describe Natalie's delusions and her fragile grasp on reality. Velma laughs when I speak of the paranoia that prevents Natalie from doing much of anything, even seeking shelter.

"She must have received a blow to the head," May suggests. "Some terrible kind of accident to the head."

"Or else she's pickled her brain with booze," Velma says. "That can do it, too. The ones who'll do anything for a drink, you know? Except an honest day's work for an honest day's pay."

I take a deep breath and try to say something about schizophrenia and the drugs that can help control it and the lack of hospital beds and the restrictions on involuntary commitment.

"It's a terrible shame," May says. "We have to write these senators. Because that health nurse said if she stays on the street she'll probably get very sick, with sores and infections and everything else. She'll probably just die on the street if she won't accept shelter."

Velma softens and clucks her tongue. No one wants to be unkind. No one knows what to say or do.

"I don't know what to do either," I say. "But not feeding her doesn't seem to be the answer."

I come upstairs without a headache, but talking about Natalie has me upset and feeling overwhelmed. I wonder what went on with that worker—not a mental health worker, I'm sure. Natalie apparently assured her that she can take care of herself. I imagine her either putting on her tough facade and refusing to talk at all or else projecting her sweet, polite, almost coherent side. The woman must have been young or inexperienced if she actually offered to take Natalie home with her. She must not have realized that she was dealing with such a delusional person. The idea that Natalie would abandon her cart and bags, travel to a public phone booth and call someone to come and pick her up to take her to a shelter that probably can't contain her anyway is absurd—rational, but absurd. I am absurd myself to keep speaking to Natalie as if this is a real option for her. I think it's just something I say now when she makes me feel desperate.

| | NOVEMBER 11

I take noodles over after work. As we're chatting, an elderly Korean man walks up behind us and stops, standing formally in his tan suit and tie until I turn to him and say hello. Natalie knits her brow and averts her eyes, displeased both by his presence and my acknowledgment of it.

"Mother?" he asks, looking first at me and then at Natalie, connecting us with a broad gesture of his hand.

"You mean, is she my mother?" I say.

"You her mother," he says, and smiles, very pleased. He may be trying to ask if I'm related to Natalie at all. Or maybe he is pointing out that I'm acting like a mother feeding her.

"Just a friend," I say. "A neighbor."

The man nods approval and smiles again, standing at ease with folded hands. He obviously wants to stay and watch and listen, mild-mannered witness to some sort of spectacle or minor calamity, but Natalie has clammed up and turns deliberately away from him.

"She's not feeling well today," I say, oddly obliged to make excuses for her. "She may not be in the mood for visitors."

The man smiles some more and nods his understanding as he moves past us. A few yards down the sidewalk, though, he stops, reaches for his wallet, and returns with a crisp dollar bill. Natalie's expression changes the instant she sees the money. Now she's all sweetness, smiling and nodding and thanking him politely, not once but several times—she already has the bill pocketed and zipped up tight, in fact, before she's finished thanking him. I pretend not to notice where she keeps her stash.

"Maybe you can eat the noodles while they're hot," I say. "Anything for me to take?"

Natalie reaches underneath her cart and hands me an unusually heavy brown paper bag. "Be careful," she warns. "It's a big B.M. in a jar."

"Oh," I say. "Great."

"It's got a lid on it, too."

"This must be our lucky day," I say.

I I NOVEMBER 12

I am home from work with a cold today and think I won't see Natalie, but by 4:30 or so I feel I can at least boil her a couple of eggs.

"Hello, hello, hello," she says cheerily as I approach. She is eating white rice from a plastic container, and she jams her plastic fork deep into it, snaps on the lid, and carefully situates the whole kit behind one rear wheel of her cart. "It's good," she says. "Good, good, good."

I am relieved to see that other people are feeding Natalie, and not junk food, either. "If you get more food tonight," I tell her, "maybe you can save the eggs for tomorrow morning."

Natalie still seems to have a slight cold but is definitely feeling better, unusually congenial, in fact, and in her limited way more coherent than usual, though everything is still couched in paranoid terms. She delights in telling me things she claims someone has told her not to tell at all, or not to tell Ann specifically. "Oh, they don't want me to tell Ann. But I had that one place, see. But I couldn't stay there unless I gave the man of the house a little pleasure. He said don't tell Ann, but don't you know how to give a man a little pleasure? I wasn't sure if you'd come today or not."

"I've been in bed all day," I tell her. "With a cold. Just when yours is better, I get one."

"Well, where did you stay in bed?" she asks. "Over across there?"

"Yes," I say. "Over there in that white building. I've been in there all day." I don't think Natalie really takes this in, because she seems to have it in her head that I live on the street as she does.

"Did he scare you yesterday?" she says. "What do you think he wanted? He sure was dressed up, wasn't he? He scared you, though. I could tell he did. What did he want? He just kept standing there talking to you. Didn't he scare you a little bit?"

"The man who gave you the money?" I ask. I can't believe we're having a conversation about a real event, albeit somewhat distorted. "He didn't scare me."

Natalie shoots me her knowing, sexually loaded smile. "Yes, he did," she insists quietly. "Yes, he did. Oh, yes. He did."

"I shooed him away like a fly," I tell her. "Not that many things scare me, really."

"Oh yes, they do," Natalie says. Her talk this evening has a different flavor, not so much pressured with a need to get something out as a need for companionship. She is even able to give me a chance to talk while she tries her best to listen. I want to stay with her, but there is a feisty breeze that is chilling me, and I feel too weak to keep standing or squatting in order to hear her.

"I can't visit long," I tell her. "I'm not warm enough out here."

"Oh dear, now," Natalie says, quite distressed. "I wish I had a jacket to give you. You need to get a jacket. You should take this." She reaches up quickly and pulls her white sweater off the top of the cart and offers it.

"No," I say, "No, no, no. You have to keep that for yourself. I have a warm place to go to."

"You need a pea coat, honey. That's the best thing out here. Get yourself a pea coat and you won't get cold. Do men ever give you anything? You have such beautiful eyes. What do you think he wanted, standing out here like that, all dressed up? He may have thought he was a little bit too good."

"He asked me if I was your mother," I tell her, and we laugh. Natalie covers her mouth like a schoolgirl, and the more she laughs, the more I laugh, until I think she's just doing it to keep me going.

"But really," she says suddenly. "How do you keep your eyes so big and round and blue?"

"I paint them on every morning," I say.

"Do you *really*?"

"No, not really," I say.

"But how do you keep them like that?"

"I don't know," I say. "They're just one of my gifts, I guess."

"Oh. But you told me that way back when I was a baby," Natalie says. "Didn't you? You told me when I was a baby. Now I remember it. Sammy Davis has a glass eye, too, you know."

"So does Peter Falk," I say. "He has a glass eye, too."

"*Really?*" Natalie feigns shock, though I get the feeling she doesn't know who I'm talking about.

"You know, Peter Falk," I say. "He used to be Columbo. The detective with the raincoat."

"You don't mean it," Natalie says. "I never heard of it. All that time and he never told me a thing about it. They blew up that whole place. Maybe it blew out his eye. They don't stop. I said it the whole time I was at the Strand, if you think anybody was listening. You don't talk enough, Ann. This lady took everything away already. I used to be able to use a cup and hit it every time, but now it goes all down the side."

"You should probably get up on your feet more," I tell her. "Get some exercise. Move around a little bit and get your circulation going."

"Oh, yes. I walked all the way up the hill and then back behind where those cans are," Natalie says. "But they tell me to stay right here, so right here I am. I'd like to change, but every time I do, these boys come around here. It doesn't take me long to change, but then people here will say there's that old so-and-so out there changing clothes."

"So a lady already took your trash?" I ask, fervently hoping that this is true.

"She took everything I had," Natalie says. "Everything. All I have left is what you see right here." We survey her sea of bags, at least twelve or fifteen by now.

"Well, it looks like enough," I say. "I think you're pretty well fixed up."

"Oh, yes," Natalie says. "If they would leave me alone for about five minutes I could straighten it all out."

"You seem to be having such a good day today," I say. "I'm glad I came over."

"Well, it's been so good to see you," Natalie says.

We've never exchanged such pleasantries, and they feel deeply soothing to me. I rise to go and am nearly across the street when Natalie draws me back, prolonging the goodbye.

"Oh, Ann, Ann, Ann," she calls. "I told you about my delicacy, didn't I?"

"No," I say, returning partway.

"Didn't I tell you about that? That delicacy?"

"I don't think so," I say. "What delicacy is that?"

"That sweet rice I used to get, with that fish skin wrapped around it. I like to have something sweet once in a while, you know. But this tasted like fish. Haven't you ever had it?"

"No," I say. "I had sushi once, though."

"This sweet, sweet rice with a fish's skin wrapped all around it," Natalie says. "You have to try it."

"I think I saw it once," I say. "But I didn't want to eat it."

"It's my delicacy, honey. It could be a favorite, in a way. They say it's awfully delicate, too, the way it's made, you know."

NATALIE ON THE STREET

I feel worse today instead of better. I wake up shivering before 6 a.m. and realize it's past time in the season to add extra quilts. Even with more covers I often wake up cold in winter because these old apartments have push-button gas heat but no thermostats. I lie with the blankets over my head, gathering courage to throw back everything and rush nude to the heat switch at the far end of the entryway. Push once and a white light comes on for "high." Push twice and it's red and white for "medium." Three times and it's red alone for "low." Push it again and you've turned it off. I push once but get no light, then remember this nuisance from last spring, the burned-out bulbs that I put off asking Mrs. Moller about. At eighty-eight she is more than slightly deaf, and by raising her voice and becoming overly involved she has a knack for turning minor problems into major confrontations, which I try to avoid if possible.

With the lights not working, you have to remember how many times you pushed or you won't be able to stop the heat without a great deal of experimentation, traveling back and forth from the switch to the living room register to test the airflow, which doesn't respond immediately, no matter what you've done. I dive back into bed and cover up everything except the tip of my nose, until the stream of warm, stale, vaguely chemical air from the basement rises sufficiently to conquer the chill. It's only in the mid-fifties, but apparently I've completed my climatic transformation from hardy midwesterner to California sissy. I drift back into a sickish sleep and wake up an hour later bathed in sweat.

No thermostat means I have to be my own, responding to changes in temperature by resetting the distant button.

Out the window, in dim, gray light, I see Natalie outlined on the sidewalk, covered from head to toe herself with the blanket-size sheet of clear, thick plastic. I think her cart and bags shield her from the wind a bit. She lies flat on her back, with only the clothes she's wearing and the furry black coat lining between her and concrete. The sight of her defeats me, and I realize I won't go to work today. There are the sniffles and the fever and the aching forehead, the lack of strength in my knees. And then there's the weakness of spirit that seems to be settling into my bones. I'm afraid I'll get to work and find the house shut up against the cold, with residents who function much better than Natalie sitting inside, chain-smoking and watching TV or going through piles of donated clothing, hoping to find something that will halfway fit, even if it isn't stylish or pretty or handsome. I'm afraid somebody in the kitchen will burn baloney and eggs in the skillet, and the odor of despair will do me in. Most days I'm happy to go but not today. Most days the fact that six people who suffer diseases like Natalie's are off the street and getting two weeks of food and shelter and psychiatric treatment is enough to cheer me on, but not today.

| | |

By noon I've had coffee and lots of orange juice and feel strong enough to call Mrs. Moller about the bulbs.

"Do you have any bulbs that fit the heat switch, Esther?" I ask, as loudly and distinctly as I can.

"What is it? What kind of bulb is it? Sidney would know. I don't know. I don't have it, whatever it is." Sidney was Mrs. Moller's husband, who died six or seven years ago, leaving her in charge of this twelve-unit building.

"Just a little bulb that goes behind the heat switch," I say. "Mine are both burned out. That's all it is."

"Oh, my god," she shouts. "I have to get the electrician again. All of a sudden you don't have heat. What next, am I right? Now. What next?"

"I have heat, I have heat. All I need is the bulbs. I can probably put them in myself if you can just get the bulbs."

"You can do this yourself, dahling? I don't think so. Are you sure? You do everything yourself, is that it? You know how this whole caboodle works? This switch, this bulb? This whatever it is?"

I feel myself fading. "I don't know for sure," I say. "I just thought if I had the bulbs I could probably try to do it."

"You're a smart girl," she says. "I get you these bulbs, you do it if you can. Now. Where do I get such bulbs? The hardware, maybe. I'll get somehow to the hardware and get you these bulbs."

"That's all right," I say. She'll have to walk or take the bus, which she is quite vigorously capable of doing, but she doesn't want to, and who can blame her? "I'll pick them up myself," I say. "I'll take the old ones with me, so I can see what to get. Then you can reimburse me."

"I can reimburse you," Esther says. "Bring me that receipt. And be careful, dahling. Thank God if you know what you're doing."

I have to lie back down for a while. I should have Mrs. Moller's spunk when I'm eighty-eight—I don't even have it at forty-three.

She does take care of this building. Eight single women besides herself live here, and three single men. She argues with all of us over everything, but she does take care of the building, and rents remain reasonable, despite her maximum allowable raises each year. She has no children and still mourns her husband. One day in the hall she more or less collapsed into my arms, weeping at the loss of him, his sheer unbearable absence. I like to be gentle with her, though she is never gentle with others, even when she's being kind. "Thank God if you know what you're doing." I haven't the slightest idea what I'm doing. I'm writing a novel that may never see print, working a job that barely covers rent and food, and somehow, after so many years in love, I seem to be ending up alone and lost. The only thing I'm sure of doing is aging, day by day.

| | |

Mid-afternoon I force myself to get up and dress and make the bed (you've made your bed, now stay out of it). I decide to go to the hardware store. Take care of something—my usual shield against the demons of panic and defeat. I drink more juice and search for a Phillips screwdriver, finally have to fashion a paper clip to unscrew the switchplate from the wall and get at the bulbs. Accomplishing this has a steadying effect.

I bundle up against the gray and windy day. On the way to my car I wave to Natalie, who is standing in position behind her cart and seems to be looking at me but doesn't respond. Natalie really does inhabit her own world in a closely defined space over there. It's as if you have to physically enter the magic circle before you can connect with her—her version of *apart*-ment.

At the hardware store I hand the man a bulb, which he holds up between thumb and forefinger. "Peanut bulb," he says. "Don't got it."

"Peanut bulb," I say. The bulb is cylindrical, and I want to ask him why it's called a peanut bulb, but I think he's in a hurry. Besides, most people don't like to be asked why something is called something—it's too often perplexing. "Do you know where I can get some?" I ask. He's writing down the name and address of an electrical supply store before the question is complete. I think the cold has thrown my timing off. I feel out of sync and don't know if I have the stamina for the twenty-minute roundtrip drive, but I do it anyway, because that seems preferable to not doing it.

The concrete building is low and flat with small window slots spaced just below the ceiling. Along the counter that runs the width of the place, several orderly lines of men wait to be served by boys who hurry to the back and disappear among aisle after aisle of mysterious merchandise. Most of the customers seem to be signing credit card receipts and putting things on account under company names, so I begin to worry that an ordinary person off the street isn't even supposed to be in here. There is a clubby feeling, and these men are speaking a language of their own. I am heartened to see one other woman present, sitting behind a computer screen on the other side of the counter. She's the one the stockboys seem most often to consult.

There is no air circulating, and by the time it's my turn I'm soaked in sweat beneath my two-too-many layers of clothing. "Do you carry these?" I ask the boy, not wanting to risk saying *peanut* when I don't know what it means.

"Peanut bulbs," he says. "How many do you need?"

"Two," I say.

"A couple dozen, then?"

"Two bulbs," I say. "Just two individual bulbs."

"I'll have to see," he says. He goes to ask the woman and she must have said yes, because he comes back with two packets, one bulb each. "Ten fifty-seven," he says. "Charge that for you?"

"Cash," I say, but find I've got only six dollars with me. Who would think light bulbs could cost so much? I also have only six dollars in checking, which is what I get for not going to work on payday. "I'll have to give you five dollars in cash and the rest in a check," I tell him.

"We can take a credit card," the boy says.

"I don't have a credit card." I watch the familiar facial response to this terrible confession—disbelief, followed by vague but dark suspicions regarding my character and personal destiny. I could back down, give up my place in line, go out into the wind, search the neighborhood for a branch of my bank and draw money out of savings, but I don't offer this.

The boy looks at me for a long moment and gives in. "OK," he says. "Go ahead."

I hand him a five and write a check for five fifty-seven.

"Jesus Christ," the man behind me sighs.

I suppress an impulse to lay my cheek flat down on the counter where I bet it's cool. The boy is consulting with the computer woman again, my check and driver's license in hand, and things don't look good. She is, in fact, yelling at him in a whispered, businesslike way. He comes back to the register near me and punches a remarkable number of buttons, but the machine responds only with annoying beeps. He repeats this procedure several times, but the thing won't cough, open out, print a receipt, or shut up. The boy returns to the woman's desk.

"Jesus H. Christ," the man behind me says out loud, and I think for spite I could pretend to faint and fall backwards right into his arms.

"It's not PROGRAMMED to accept cash and check in the same transaction," the woman announces to everyone. "Ring the goddam totals up SEPARATELY."

The boy returns red-faced, quickly accomplishes two receipts, and calls out "Next" as he thrusts them into my hand, which keeps me from apologizing.

"Jeez," the man behind me says as he steps up to the counter. "Gimme a break, huh?"

Back home I sit in the car for a few minutes, chilly but too wrung out to dash for the building just yet. I gave Natalie a short honk and waved as I drove by, but she just stared, unrecognizing if she heard at all. She is sitting huddled against her cart, her jacket zipped all the way up, the blue cap pulled all the way down. Probably "responding to internal stimuli," as they say in the biz. I can't go over there yet.

I try to sneak past Mrs. Moller's door, but she must have noticed me coming in—suddenly there she is, a feisty old bulldog in a great burst of commotion. I summon up the patience these encounters always require.

"Where did you go, did you go to the hardware? Did you get it? What is it? Can I see? Let me see. Can you fix it? You think you can fix it? Let me see what is it. How much was it? You had to have two? You got two of them already, huh? Come in, come in, come in."

I don't want to go in. I want her to let me deduct the money from my rent, but she won't hear of it.

"That's not the way things are done, dahling. Then everyone gets confused." We sit at her kitchen formica table, underneath an astonishing glass chandelier that could kill us both if it fell. Esther has one of those thick, flat, notebook-style checkbooks, each check with its own carbon, and she has a pen light, that is, a pen with a light on it, which she shines on the receipts as she holds them under a small magnifying glass. "Two receipts," she says. "Two bulbs, two receipts. What is that?"

"It's ten fifty-seven total," I say, not wanting to shout an explanation.

"So. You're the genius electrician today. This is very good, Ann. This is very good, believe me. You're a smart girl. But I tell you what. You have to look out for yourself, not the others. They will only break your heart. I'm telling you this. You can't change people into what you want them to be. Your kind of help is not always the help they need, and this is the hardest lesson. I'm telling you this for your own good. Because I had to learn it the hard way myself."

I'm not sure whether this is just something she needs to get said or if she is suggesting, in her own inimitable way, that I quit helping Natalie.

"People live their lives the way they live their lives. Sometimes it's a very sad thing. This is what I'm telling you. You can try till you're blue in the face, or whatever you want to call it. Look out for yourself, dahling. This is what I'm saying to you. And it's the hardest lesson, believe me. Take it from someone who knows."

I mutter in agreement but decide to lie low. I'm not about to get into a discussion of Natalie while concealing the filthy, filthy secret that I stash her feces in Mrs. Moller's garbage bins several times a week. Of course Esther may know that, too, since cataracts don't affect the sense of smell. She labors to fill in the date and my name on the check. Esther is German and has no trouble spelling it. She looks up at me before writing the amount.

"So," she says. "No husband yet."

"No husband," I say.

"Germans, I don't know," she says. "German husbands are no good. Too demanding. They want to boss the woman."

"Oh, I don't know," I say. "I was married to a German. He was a good man. He was a good husband." It occurs to me I've now been unmarried for eleven years, the same length of time I was married. For some reason this strikes me as a staggering statistic. I've lived alone, even through relationships with women, for as long as I ever lived with a mate.

"Latins are the worst," Esther is saying. "The woman to them is nothing. Jewish is best. Like my Sidney. Why? Because they are taught. The mothers teach their little boys to treat girls right. 'Don't hit your sister, don't push your sister, aren't you ashamed?' A Jewish man is the best to women. He respects a woman. This is true. You look around and see if it's not so."

My right eye begins to tear copiously, and I have to get up and reach for a paper towel.

"What is it, dahling, what, what?"

"Just my eye is running," I say.

"You did what?"

"MY EYE IS RUNNING," I shout. "I HAVE A COLD."

"I have lemons," Esther says. "They come right off the tree, don't worry about it." She gets up and extracts three slightly brown lemons from her refrigerator, sets them in my lap and sits back down to sign the check. "*And,*" she says. "Now they have proven that Jews don't get AIDS. It's because of the circumcision."

"No, Esther," I say. "That isn't true."

"Yes, it's so, it's so. Because it's cleaner. An uncircumcised man, he has that skin, and the bacteria get in there. I mean, he can't help it. But a Jewish man? No." She hands me the check, and I take it and the lemons and the peanut bulbs and head quickly for the door.

"So find yourself a good Jewish man," she calls up the stairway behind me.

"Such a good Jewish man might prefer a Jewish woman," I suggest. "Don't you think he would?"

"It's not that you're Jewish," Esther says, very much the authority on this. "It's not that you're Jewish. It's not your looks. It's not how smart you are."

"Well, what is it, then?" I say.

"It's how you can connive to catch them!" she declares, hands on hips. "That's all it is. How you connive to catch them!"

Upstairs, defeated and depleted, I lie across the bed and have a short, minimally cathartic cry.

| | |

After a nap I install the damn bulbs, not without some difficulty with connections, and turn the heat on high. It is already dark at 4:30 and starting to rain. I turn off the kitchen light and try to see Natalie out the window. I think she's lying flat again, snuggled among her bags with the plastic cover spread over her and them. It looks like she has another sheet of plastic over her cart, which is piled much higher now than when she first settled here. I know she has blankets, and maybe even other bedding in there, and for a moment I think I can go over and see if she will let me help her make a warmer, drier pallet. Instead I light my oven and put us each a potato in. I keep standing at the darkened window, watching the rain blow around the streetlight, watching for signs of movement in Natalie's camp. When the potatoes are done, I find that I can't eat mine and can't deliver hers. I light a candle in every room but have to give up early and go to bed. Natalie's been with me all day long—all the livelong day, as my mother used to say—and she's finally done me in.

Had she survived to see it, my mother would no doubt find this life I live bewildering. She wanted me to graduate from high school, go on to college, and be able to type well enough to support myself—no small ambitions considering her own eighth-grade, country-schoolhouse education and her dependent, house-bound marriage. She bought me a Smith-Corona my junior year as well as my graduation Elgin watch, knowing she'd not be around by then. I've done all the things she wanted me to and plenty more I'm sure she didn't. Getting older I feel the loss of her in a different way, not just her not knowing me grown up but of my never having known her either, for herself outside of mother. I do know she'd be feeding Natalie. I can hear her justifying the expense to my father in southern tones: "You may not know who she's kin to, but she's kin to *somebody*, now, you know that."

A beautiful day, very windy but sunny, clean and clear after the rain. Early afternoon I put the potatoes in to warm and decide I will splurge and have sour cream if the Mexican market will take Mrs. Moller's check. Natalie has been up and down all morning, fussing with her arrangement of bags and the clothing that blows about on top of her cart.

"She came here feeling around after dark last night," Natalie informs me by way of greeting. "I wasn't awake and I said, is that you, Ann, and she said, who's Ann? I don't know what she was looking for. She doesn't like me to have these things, see, and she thinks she can just take whatever she wants."

"Were you able to keep dry?" I ask, and Natalie launches into a long and convoluted description of the technicalities involved in getting her plastic cover situated just right for rain and especially for wind. I gather that the wind was blowing up under it, no matter what she tried. She seems confused but at the same time oriented enough to know that the heavy winds began this morning after daybreak, not during the night.

"I'm afraid of that wind when it gets too close to the ground," she whispers. "It can do you a lot of damage."

"How do you feel about sour cream?" I say.

"Sour cream? How I feel about it? Cottage cheese with some peaches wouldn't be half bad, either, would it?"

"I mean I'm baking a potato," I say. "Would you care for a baked potato?"

"Oh, yes," Natalie says. "I would care for one if you have one, sure. Why, certainly. I don't use too much salt, you know. That salt you gave me, I have that. It's got the Colonel on it. But I don't use too much. It makes you thirsty and then it's trouble."

She has kept track of a miniature packet of salt I gave her weeks ago with eggs. "I won't put salt on it, then," I tell her. "But how about butter and pepper? Or how about sour cream if I can get us some sour cream?"

"Oh yes," Natalie says. "Oh yes, oh yes, oh yes. I eat mine with the peeling and all. I mean, if you have the peeling on it. Of course, some don't, if it's more refined or whatever. How much cream do you put on yours? You know, she kept asking me, who's Ann, who's Ann, who's Ann. I don't know what she wanted with you, but you better watch out. Keep your eye on the where-abouts." She nods, not turning, toward the house behind her.

Natalie rests both hands on the handle of her cart, and I stand facing her as if we're having this chat in a grocery aisle. We are both a bit the worse for wear—Natalie has a black smudge all across her forehead below her cap line and looks as if she could use a good night's sleep. I've got a red nose, a teary eye, and cramps on top of the cold today.

"I'll just put your sour cream on the side," I tell her. "I'll put it beside your potato, and then you can use as much as you want. I'll leave the peeling on it. I have to go to the store." I turn away abruptly to get out of the wind. Halfway across the street I think this may have seemed rude to her, but when I look back she is still standing and staring exactly as she was, not in the least ac-knowledging my departure. *I don't hear voices,* she told me. *But I do have trouble with people disappearing.*

The corner market is full of Saturday bustle, but Mercedes takes the check, as usual, with no I.D., because I'm in there often and none so far has bounced. The cottage cheese and peaches are a good idea, though I won't buy them today. I get the potato doctored up on a paper plate and take it out steaming hot with a complete utensil packet from Colonel Sanders: a small, rectangular bag that contains a plastic spoon-fork, a paper napkin, a pack of salt, and a moist towelette, all of which please Natalie immensely.

"I use these all the time," she says. "These moist towelettes. Every chance I get."

"I'll bring you a bunch of them," I say. I actually have a drawer full of the things, left over from months of visiting the Colonel but refusing to eat out of the box with plastic (one has to draw the line to keep oneself "refined"—real plates and real silverware, even if the food's not real). Natalie is sitting on her bed, and I can tell by the way she holds onto the potato that she wants me to leave so she can eat. "Catch you later," I say.

"Thank you," Natalie says. "I love these potatoes like this, don't you?"

Today I can eat and read. I'm nearly finished re-reading all of Joan Didion, fiction and nonfiction. She is either the best or worst companion to choose for a dark season. In "On Morality" she pares that concept of all its potential hypocrisy and mendacity and winds up with one stark and irrefutable image:

"Whether or not a corpse is torn apart by coyotes may seem only a sentimental consideration, but of course it is more: one of the promises we make to one another is that we will try to retrieve our casualties, try not to abandon our dead to the coyotes. If we have been taught to keep our promises—if, in the simplest terms, our upbringing is good enough—we stay with the body, or have bad dreams."

| | NOVEMBER 15

Another clear and sunny day after a windy, chilly night, down to 50°. I was cold inside under blankets, so I know Natalie couldn't have been warm enough, though the heavy plastic she lies under does keep out air if she can get it anchored right.

"Were you cold last night?" I ask.

"Oh, yes," she says matter-of-factly. "Yes, I was cold, all right."

"You have blankets in your cart," I start in, but she shoots me the look that indicates this is not to be a subject for discussion today. She gazes up at the things I've brought: a plastic container with lid, in the hope she can defecate in it; tissues and wet-naps, in the hope she can wipe; a clean pair of underpants, in the hope she will change; a double brown bag inside a plastic one, to carry away whatever she'll give me; and three boiled eggs and a small banana. Natalie surprises me by peeling back the banana immediately and gumming away with intense concentration, finishing it before we speak again.

She is talkative today, much of it the usual rambling about being beaten and about "him" sticking it into her bowel. "I mean his *joint*, Ann, right up in the bowel so that whatever comes out comes out. You could call, you could scream, or not, because he won't give a you-know-what what you do, anyway, if he likes it or doesn't like it or calls you every name in the book doesn't matter. If you talk back is when they got out that pipe. But I used to get those coupons and try to use them at the store, you know, but it never quite worked out, really, for some reason, they would always come back and throw everything out in your face, anyway. I was wearing a shawl at that time, you know, which the dearest of friends had knitted my name on. So of course the other girls were jealous of that and wanted nothing but trouble."

However hard you listen to Natalie, it's impossible to follow or anticipate her train of thought. She can jabber on and on this way until the words seem to evaporate before they reach your brain. At one point deep inside an impossible story, she mentions slipping some food into a bread wrapper, which I mistake for a "red rubber."

"*What?*" I say. "Into a red rubber? Really?" I laugh, and Natalie gets a twinkle in her eye and says no, *bread wrappers*.

"But them red rubbers, that was something, too, wasn't it? Over there on Sixth Street. Right around Union there. Up under that carport—cases and cases of them red rubbers. It was kind of interesting, but my goodness, I'd never seen such a thing before. But oh, honey, some of the things some of them would do, you wouldn't even believe. They wouldn't even believe it in confession, I'm telling you. They locked me in that incinerator over there, and the only way I could get out was by praying. The officer said, how in the world did you get in here? You don't know how terrible some people can be, honey."

A little Black boy, seven or eight, in a Dodger cap, stops at the curb on his bike to announce a yard sale his mother is having over on the next street. "You wanna come over there?" he asks us both. "Don't you wanna come over there and see it?" He is excited in a genuine kid-like way, something I don't often see, and I tell him I may stop over later.

"Thanks for telling us," I say, but Natalie is angry and frightened, even raising her voice to shoo the child away. "It's all right," I say. "He's just talking about a yard sale."

"They're the ones who come around here after dark and get into my things," Natalie says, suddenly hawking and spitting onto the grass near my feet. "They try to find out everything I have, and then they want to sell it. You don't even know what you're talking about."

The boy peddles off slowly, and I feel bad for him, for the sweetness and openness in him that already needs protection. Natalie and I don't exchange parting words.

On my way across the street, May calls out for me to stop and wait for her. May, who told me to quit "encouraging" Natalie, appears to be on her way home from church. "Blessed are the merciful," she says, "for they shall obtain mercy."

"Hey, I hope so," I laugh. "Mercy me."

May smiles, too, and her face is gentle, really a Sunday morning kind of face—a small-town, gray-eyed, churchy kind of face beneath white hair and a devil-may-care red tam.

"I've been praying hard for this woman," she says, nodding in Natalie's direction. "And I mentioned you in my prayers, too, this morning."

Something in me cringes at this, and almost, for a moment, takes offense. Suspicions rise. What makes her think she has to pray for me along with Natalie? I thank her, though, and as I thank her I feel that I mean it and am able to accept what must be intended. It occurs to me I could say a prayer for May as well, or maybe thinking of it is a prayer in itself.

May's concern for Natalie has increased now that she knows she's not just a stubborn, filthy old bum who lives and behaves as she does by choice.

"This kind of thing shouldn't exist in America," she keeps saying, shaking her head. She is asking people at her church to write letters to the government. "But she's set for food, at least, isn't she?" May seems to think that Natalie's bags are full of groceries and is dismayed to learn this isn't so. She aims to go straight to the store for bread, but I tell her the buns from the Mexican market may be too hard for someone without teeth. We agree on the beauty of eggs, and then May settles on the idea of juices in containers that don't require an opener.

"Or a gallon of water," I suggest. "Maybe if she has that much on hand she'll drink some in spite of herself."

May voices her constant worry that Natalie will be slain or "abused" on the street. This woman turns out to be an avid crime buff, full of grisly tales of rape and murder and mutilation.

"Some of the serial killers, you know, concentrate exclusively on street people. I mean the women especially. The vagrants. And the prostitutes, of course. Somebody downtown right now is cutting these poor people with a razor while they sleep. Did you read about that at all? Cutting throats but also cutting the women on their chests. This is the kind of thing that goes on every day, and most of it doesn't even make the paper. We had one years and years ago who was slicing eyebrows off to put in his knapsack."

May would go on in this vein for a very long time, but I am sneezing and tell her I have to get in out of the wind.

"Well, you call up that woman from the Social Service. See what she has to say. The only thing is, I didn't get her name. Of course, I didn't give her my name, either. I would never want to be responsible for having someone committed, you know."

"I'm going to make some calls," I tell her. "To check and see if there is anything Natalie might be able to take advantage of. There used to be a van on the westside that brought food and clothes around and had a shower on board. But they may have lost their funding by now. I don't know if they would come this far downtown, anyway."

"I bet you're one of these people like my grandmother who just does for other people until you get sick," May says.

"No, I'm not," I tell her. "I really am not, believe me." It might shock May, in fact, to learn how selfish I can be.

| | |

My *Book of Common Prayer* now has one For Those Who Live Alone. We've become a category of persons, like The Oppressed, The Poor and Neglected, The Unemployed, The Victims of Addiction, or Those Who Suffer for the Sake of Conscience. *(And God help, most especially, intransigent souls who choose to live alone. Strengthen us in our several necessities.)* I guess Those in Mental Darkness includes the Natalies of this world. Praying was the only way she got out of that incinerator.

| | NOVEMBER 16

About four o'clock I take Natalie Instant Lunch, which comes in its own styrofoam cup. I tell her it's noodles with shrimp, and she is very pleased although, not believing there can be shrimp, she has to poke around in the broth until she confirms it to her satisfaction.

"Won't you have a Pepsi?" she offers, pointing to a small white styrofoam cooler sitting camouflaged among her bags. "I got two of 'em in there."

"No, thanks," I say. "Who brought you the cooler?"

"That man in the truck. He comes around in that truck. I hate to talk about anybody." Natalie's tone slides into a whispered caricature of confidentiality. "I hate to talk about somebody, you know, but I don't much like that man. I truly don't."

"Well, it was nice of him to bring you the cooler, anyway," I say. "You'll be able to keep other things in it, too."

"What did you do today?" she asks, so directly that I feel a combination of embarrassment and guilt.

"Not much," I say. "I'm still sick with the flu or something. My brain feels like cottonballs."

"You have that hood," she says, referring to my sweatshirt. "That's a good idea. What day is it?"

This is a startling question, coming from Natalie, who ordinarily exhibits a firm indifference to "real" time and space. "It's Monday, November 16," I tell her, and aloud this sounds like a remarkable piece of information.

"I don't like to say anything," Natalie says, thoroughly conversational. "But this flu bug seems to be going around. I think people might be caught up in the bustle between Halloween and Thanksgiving. That's one thing I have known."

"Maybe so," I say. Exactly my problem, caught up in the bustle between Halloween and Thanksgiving.

"People try to cram too much into too little time," Natalie goes on. "There's too much to do and not enough time to do it in. You know that container you brought for me to keep? Well, she took it."

"I brought it for you to go to the bathroom in," I say.

"Well, I did, but it was only half full. My sister used to try to send me to the store before breakfast, even. And then she'd say, oh, *you* set the table, Nattie, *you* do it better than anyone."

We share a modest laugh about people who try to get you to do the work by telling you that you do it best. Natalie likes to laugh, or maybe I'm the one who likes it so much when she laughs. There is something inherently sane about most laughter that is always a deep source of comfort to me.

"Of course, you know I was raped in a field by my father's best friend," Natalie continues. "But my father told them all, don't you ever say Natalie can't serve herself at the table. He says, she works harder in the field than anybody. See, because at the time I was doing Becky's work and Emily's too."

"Where was the farm?" I ask. "In California?"

"Midwest," she says. "Kansas, Missouri, Nebraska. Around in there. But then them big wops. Italian guys, you know. And I bought that fish that made my dad mad. He said why buy that fish and pay that money when we had it at home. But these two guys weighed about 850 pounds. I had to call them up on the phone, see."

"You're full of so many tales," I say. "I really can't keep up with you."

"What day did you say it was?"

"Monday, November 16," I repeat.

"And when is Thanksgiving, then?" Natalie asks. "There isn't that much time to get ready, I don't think."

"Thanksgiving will be on the 26th," I say. "So it's only a week and a half away."

"That queer that gave me eight dollars down at the Chinese place on Union, too," Natalie says. "I mean he was *queer*, honey.

I don't like to say what he told me to buy. Maybe it was Miracle Whip or something. He may have needed something for his lettuce, I don't know. But as soon as I left, he beat the other guy up. It was an important person, too. I don't like to say who it was, but it was in all the headlines the next morning. That was when we still had different papers, you know."

"Better eat the soup while it's warm," I suggest. Not far from where she set the soup is another cup, half covered with a piece of clear plastic and a narrow shred of newspaper, buzzing with flies. I will have to take this to my car, where I'm keeping a supply of bags, and wrap it extra tight for disposal. Then I'll scrub my hands twice, up to the elbow. "Listen, Natalie," I say. "Did you happen to get a chance to put on that underwear I brought?"

"Oh, yes," she says. "I put them on right over the others, so it'll soak up that seepage."

| | NOVEMBER 17

The day is gray with rain predicted. I take Natalie eggs and a bran muffin around 11:00, before going to the library. I think she is dozing when I approach, though she always tries to act as if she isn't. When I ask how she feels, she says she didn't sleep well, that there were police down the street and a plane (she must mean helicopter) flying around. Most likely this is true.

"I didn't go to sleep till daylight," she whispers. "Of course I had to hold what was in me while they were around."

I ask if she has any garbage, and she says no.

"Anything at all for me to take?"

She hesitates, looks at me, says no again. I get the feeling she doesn't want to wear me out carrying stuff away for her. I know there is at least one other woman in the neighborhood who helps with this, and there are several of us who bring food, though our efforts are not organized.

These days Natalie lies/sleeps/sits with her head against the bottom of the shopping cart, no kind of pillow. This remarkable tolerance for discomfort, or what most people would experience as discomfort, enables her to spend her days and nights on concrete without complaint. There has been dried blood on her left cheek for several days now, a fairly deep scratch or scrape that she won't admit to or discuss. This lowered sensitivity to pain may look like a blessing but could be dangerous. Whenever she mentions abdominal pain I feel as if it must be severe in order for her to bring it up.

"Don't you have a Medi-Cal card or something?" I always ask, and she says yes, but only in the vaguest of tones, as if having one is irrelevant, if indeed she does have one.

"If you feel sick, just tell me," I say. "I'll get the paramedics out here, and you can go to a hospital. Maybe that's what we should do. You think?"

"I have all that," Natalie says. "Give it over and they'll stick it right down your throat. I don't like to show my identification. They cut off whatever it is they don't like."

I offer to bring a warm washcloth over so she can wipe off her face and neck.

"I've already washed this morning, honey," she lies. "Everything but combed my hair. *Your* hair sure looks pretty." She does a kind of double take then, leans on her elbow and brings her face right up to mine as I squat beside her. "You just look *beauti-*

ful," she says, so sincerely I realize I've been feeling ugly for weeks. "How do you make yourself so *beautiful*?" There is awe in her voice, as if I'm a star with secrets to reveal, though I haven't done a thing but wash my hair—no make-up, not even lipstick or earrings today.

"It's just me," I tell her, rising. "Here I am—TA-DA!" I do the little singsong of stage announcement and stamp my foot, and Natalie opens her mouth for a toothless laugh, which quickly fades.

"TA-DA, huh?" Her tone insinuates there may have been something salacious in my behavior, and she eyes me with suspicion, as if I might be a stripper about to disrobe.

"We could wash your hair, Natalie," I say suddenly. "It would be beautiful. What about it? I mean, it's too cold today, but what about a sunny day? I'll bring a bucket, and you lean over so I can pour it on your head, and then while you shampoo I'll get another bucketful to rinse with. You can rub it with a towel and then dry it in the sun. What do you think? Then you'll look beautiful, too."

Natalie seems amused by all this and adopts an air of tolerance toward my enthusiasm. "You know, honey," she says, sweet but firm, "my hair doesn't get dirty. That's why I wear this cap. That's why they tell me to keep it on, whatever else I do. This hair used to get dirty when I was younger, but it doesn't get that dirty anymore. As long as I comb it every day is all it needs."

| | |

At dinner, around 7:00, I have a few bites of take-out Armenian chicken left, so I tear it up and take it to Natalie, with mostly tomatoes from the salad along with a piece of pita. Pocket bread, she calls it, when I ask if she can chew it. Pocket bread, exactly right. It is raining, and I am in my hooded sweatshirt.

"Oh, did you get wet?" Natalie asks. "I hope you don't get wet out here." She lies underneath the plastic sheet with all her garbage bags, and the odor is thick and damp as she rises up on her elbow. She seems unusually gladdened by the food tonight.

"Can you eat under there?" I ask, and she says yes, grunting and laughing a bit because it is very awkward to try to stay arranged so that the plastic covers her while she holds the plate and tries to eat and keep the food dry, too.

Maybe I can manage another "bath" this weekend if the weather is warm enough and I'm feeling up to it and Natalie will cooperate.

| | NOVEMBER 18

Just past 7:00 this morning I stop by to speak to Natalie as I return from running. I approach from the street instead of along the sidewalk behind her. Sometimes I think she doesn't like to be approached from the street. She is hostile and has on her angry face, not sweet and not receptive. Although she asks if I've been running, she acts as if it's a silly thing to do, which I suppose it is from her perspective. An Asian man, in shirtsleeves and tie, walks by us on the sidewalk side, careful not to look our way.

"He's a creep," Natalie says aloud before he's all the way past. "You wouldn't know to look at him, but he is. He comes along here with his wife and two kids, and he thinks with the four of them they can take anything they want."

There is an obvious accumulation of feces on a newspaper nearby, with many, many flies abuzz. I look at it but don't say anything because I have no bag. Maybe it's not a good idea to make such an early visit, before coffee and juice—too unsettling to the stomach.

"I guess I'll have to use my new bag," Natalie says resentfully, eyeing me eyeing the mess. From under her cart she jerks out the plastic bag I gave her last week.

"Good idea," I say, not moving, not wanting to say or do anything to agitate her further. She grabs up all the brown-covered debris, including a big wad of newspaper and a tall cup with a lid on it, and shoves it into the bag, muttering and complaining all the while that she needs more bags. She has it in her head to organize all her things and redistribute them into new, clean bags, but she doesn't have the bags. This is an ongoing preoccupation with her, and there is a kind of unspoken insinuation here that the reason she doesn't have extra bags is that I am always taking them away from her. I decide to let this lie and not protest. I'm fairly sure that if I gave her a bunch of bags she would hoard them and not reorganize, anyway. As it is now at the grocery store, however little I buy, I always ask for double bags and can't ever keep enough on hand.

Flies are still buzzing around the spot Natalie has cleared on the grass, which looks as if it's been poisoned. She should move at least a few feet away from the residue, but I'm not about to suggest that today. Suddenly she's in the middle of a rant.

"I told her to get the damn dog away from me. She walks that goddamn flea-bitten dog right up in my face and stands there like I want to talk to her or something. I talked to her all right. I told her to get that damn dog away from here scratching fleas and not to bring no more flies around here. I don't need it, need it, need it." From nowhere Natalie pulls a rotten banana peel and flourishes it like a sword. She starts to put it in the bag, then jams it into her jacket pocket instead. "I'll mash it down on that creep's desk when he isn't looking," she whispers.

As I leave I take the bag from her and hold it open until she finally, reluctantly, deposits the peeling.

"Take it, then," she calls after me bitterly. "Go ahead and take it. It's not even halfway full yet."

Not a good day for Natalie after a night of chilly mist. Sometimes the issue of bags seems more important in her mind than the issue of food. The bags represent her domain—she can control what's in the bags, if nothing else. Really she has no say-so about what food comes her way. She has the power to refuse it, but if she's hungry that power is undermined. And while she appears to be in charge of what she wears, I think her relationship to clothing and cleanliness is very much at the mercy of her paranoia. The burgundy sweatshirt that Joyce next door gave me for her, the one Natalie promised to put on but didn't, remains prominently displayed beside her on the sidewalk, not tucked away into a bag or stuffed into the cart, like other items of clothing she doesn't wear. Sometimes I feel as if this must carry a special significance, though I'm unsure what it might be.

From my kitchen window I see people cross the street to avoid Natalie's corner. People in cars slow down to look at her, then drive on.

| | NOVEMBER 19

As I leave for work I take Natalie a cup of coffee, painfully aware
that I didn't take her anything at all yesterday. She is sitting up
as I approach.

"Oh, coffee!" she cries out, raising her hands as if in praise.
Today she is smiling. "You look like you've been sleeping," she
tells me.

"I slept all night, and now I'm on my way to work," I say.

"Oh," Natalie says. "You have an apple, I see. I ate mine yesterday."

"I didn't think you could eat apples," I say. "I thought they'd
be too hard for you to chew."

"I waited till it softened up," she says. "It had gotten all brown."
She makes a motion like she is holding an apple and digging
into it with her fingers, which must be the way she ate it.

"Maybe bananas and oranges are better for you," I suggest. "I
mean, they're softer, so you can eat them while they're fresh."

"Bananas are awfully good," she says. "You have a *Newsweek*."

I am carrying a rolled-up magazine to give away at work. The
idea that Natalie might be able to spend part of her day reading
pleases me enormously. "Do you want it?" I ask. "Please take it.
I'm done with it."

"Oh, no, you keep it," she says, but when I hold it out she
accepts it and thanks me.

As I head for my car I pass a young Latino who seems hesitant
to walk by Natalie's camp. "Does she live there?" he asks, with a
tinge of disbelief.

"I'm afraid she does," I say.

"She does, huh? She lives there?" He lets out a short laugh

that is not a laugh so much as a signal that this is a very strange and sad situation. He takes to the gutter and cuts a wide circle past Natalie, shaking his head as he goes.

| | |

It is nearly dark when I take soup around 5:00, and although Natalie is in the process of sitting up as I approach, she barely acknowledges me. She pulls several times at her plastic sheet, but this appears to be a random gesture, without purpose. "It looks like cheese when you pull it up," she says, as if to explain, but I don't understand what she means at all. In the late twilight her face is gray and drawn, and she mutters several phrases I can't quite hear and don't understand except for "Boy, *he* sure left here in a hurry," repeated several times. I get the feeling she was deeply involved in her "other world" when I came up and couldn't make the transition to my presence quickly enough, or didn't want to right then, like being awakened during a dream. The magazine is nowhere in sight, and this morning's lucidity has receded into the distant past. She mutters and fusses but does eventually take the soup and manage a thank you.

I have brought her a plastic bag and two brown sacks, which she grabs and examines carefully, almost painstakingly, all the while mumbling over them as if conducting a ritual.

"This might come in handy," she concludes, and stashes the bags under her legs inside the plastic sheet. She doesn't seem to want company and in fact doesn't seem to notice when I leave.

On my way in I pass Velma downstairs. "Been out for your stroll?" she asks, as if I am one to stroll.

"Just taking some soup to our neighbor," I say.

Velma laughs at this. "I guess that old gal thinks it's her apartment over there," she says.

"Well, I guess it is her apartment," I say.

We both laugh, but coming up the stairs I'm sorry I laughed with Velma because, while I was laughing with her, she was laughing at Natalie. Velma is always getting packets of information from right-wing groups, packets too large to fit into our mailboxes, so I see them stacked on the floor below—Coalitions for this and Citizens for that (Patriotism, Democracy, and A Better America). Today it was the National Rifle Association. Several of us in the building have been burglarized by Black and Hispanic kids, but Velma was burglarized by a Caucasian male adult in a gray, three-piece suit and tie! I saw him exiting her apartment that morning, gently closing the door behind him, and then we greeted each other politely. When I heard she'd been robbed, I wrote a full description and took it down to her. Velma accepted the piece of paper, but to this day believes I was mistaken and doesn't trust what I say.

"It's a pretty sight when your own home isn't safe anymore," she kept saying. "We've come to a pretty pass now, haven't we, when they can come right into your home like that." I know that *they* is a code word for her meaning anyone not Caucasian.

Still, it's fair to say that Velma has accepted Natalie as a neighbor, at least to the extent that she has not called the police or tried to shoo her away. For the most part, in fact, people in the neighborhood have been amazingly tolerant. Two or three of us feed Natalie regularly, but many passersby stop on their way from the corner market to give her snacks or fruit or beverages. These acts of charity don't keep Natalie from seeking shelter, which I'm convinced she would not do in any case, but they do allow her the luxury of having "a place of her own" for a while rather than wandering in desperation with her cart. I see caring people set down their offerings and quickly back away. The specter of madness and destitution haunts and terrifies us all.

| | NOVEMBER 20

I take coffee again as I leave for work. Natalie has her hand inside her shirt as I approach but jerks it out when she sees me. "I put some Mercurochrome on that arm," she says.

"What happened to it?" I ask. I see no sign of either medicine or injury.

"I burned it," Natalie says. "He bit it."

"Who bit it?"

"The big guy," Natalie says. "That Joseph Kametsky. You remember him? Over there at Nelson Framing. And there was that little boy in MacArthur Park, you know. It's not MacArthur Park but Lafayette Park. He came right to me because I had packages. Children will do that, you know, if you have packages, to get something to eat. And I said, THAT HOST BELONGS IN THAT CHILD, AND YOU SEE THAT HE GETS IT. But they took his picture in the nude."

"Well, you're wearing some pretty lipstick this morning," I say.

"Am I?" Natalie says, as if she didn't know, though the lipstick, a nice, deep pink, is fresh and well applied and looks normal for a change. She keeps talking to me as I walk away, but I can't get the gist of anything.

"Happy Friday," I say. "I'm late to work."

"SHHHHHHHHH!" She waves at me with one hand and shushes me with the other, pressing a finger to her lips.

"JOE," she yells. "Hey, JOE!"

I hurry to my car and don't look back.

                    I I I

Around 5:00 I take two bran muffins and some chocolate pudding because it's all I have to take. Natalie seems glad for the sweets, though.

The smell is worse than usual, rising up from under the plastic. One of the double brown bags I brought is sitting beside her, folded down at the top, and I ask if she wants me to take it.

"Well, it's not quite full yet," she says. "There's room for some more in it. I want to put some banana peels in it. Don't bother with it now."

I am tired tonight and lack the stamina to coax or insist. All at once I feel viscerally repelled by her physical presence—the odor, the filth, the whole idea of her is unbearable, and I have to get away.

I I NOVEMBER 21

About 4 a.m. I am awakened by dogs barking and what sounds like a man and woman having a loud argument, not an unusual occurrence for the Mexican couple in the house behind me. After listening for a few moments, though, I realize it's not Spanish

I'm hearing. So many dogs are barking so loudly that it's difficult to catch the words, and not until there is a long wave of
maniacal laughter do I realize it's Natalie making all the noise,
carrying on an obscene monologue (or dialogue) in her deep,
macho, aggressive voice and her high-pitched, whiny, girl-child
voice, both at full volume. Whatever the pitch, all the obscenities are aimed at trying to keep someone away. It's goddamn this
and goddamn that, don't you this and don't you that. Natalie is
out of control, but the theme is familiar: *Right in my asshole, you
goddamn son of a bitch. Get away from my goddamn ass. I'm a white
person, you goddamn fucking bastard shitass. Keep out of that goddamn
hole if you know what's good for you before I blow your fucking head
off.* Natalie begins to squeal and cackle at such a high pitch that
the dogs start to howl as well as bark.

Stark raving mad, I keep thinking. This is what's meant by *stark
raving mad,* and my mind will not let go of the phrase, at once so
facile and brutal. At the window I press my face to the screen,
shivering in the damp chill, and I see that Natalie is indeed alone,
standing behind her cart, poised to roll away except that she is
holding forth with her head thrown back.

Suddenly many sirens erupt close by. It sounds like fire en-
gines and police cars and ambulances all at once, on Western or
Third Street north of here. The dogs—I had no idea there were
so many dogs in the neighborhood—intensify their yapping and
howling until the effect is comic, in spite of Natalie's dreadful
state. I wonder if someone has called the police on her, which
would be a blessing if they could get her hospitalized. More likely,
the police would just threaten her and tell her she has to move
on. Even if they arrested her, after the paperwork and rigmarole

she'd be back on the street by morning. This lady may be stark raving mad, but she hasn't yet tried to kill herself or anyone else, so there'd be no room in the inn tonight.

Natalie must think the sirens are for her, too, because all of a sudden she's quiet. *You shut up* is the last thing she yells. No doubt she has been to jail or been lectured by police before, so even at her worst she will attempt to avoid this. After several minutes the sirens die down, and Natalie remains quiet. It takes much longer for the dogs to settle, but at last there is silence except for sporadic barking in the distance, on and off, back and forth, for twenty or thirty minutes.

| | |

Around noon I take three eggs and a plastic bag for garbage. The sun is white-hot, and Natalie sits on the bare sidewalk, steaming and stewing, flies aswarm.

"How are you, Natalie?" I ask gently. She looks gray and exhausted, wiping sweat from each eyebrow onto a dirty sleeve.

"Nothing is any different," she says. For the first time she won't take the food from my hands but tells me to set the eggs on the sidewalk or on a sweater. "I'm not eating as much as I was," she says, "but she brought me breakfast. They don't want me to have everything." There is a resignation, a weariness in her voice that I've not heard before. She seems to think it will be very bad luck if she touches the eggs.

"You can eat them anytime you want to," I tell her. "Even tomorrow, if you don't want them today. Or you don't have to eat them at all."

NATALIE ON THE STREET |

Natalie smiles at this and thanks me, as if it's a great relief.

"Did you have a rough night?" I ask. "I heard you yelling out here last night."

"They turned over the cart again," she says, though the cart stands undisturbed beside her. "They come around here, I'm telling you. That's what *she* wanted to know, her and her flea-bitten old dog. What were you dreaming about and what are you thinking about and what are you feeling and this and that. I want to cry but can't. That's what I told that Jennifer Ryan, to get a scratch pad. You know, a scratch pad? She didn't know what a scratch pad was. This fellow I used to work for, in his office, I'm telling you. See, he hit me so hard it knocked me up against the cart, and now I'm sore on this whole side. That's what he can't understand, why I don't get up and dance. But I have to be careful because of all these kids on these milk cartons."

Natalie reaches into a garbage bag and shows me an empty pint carton of milk, which has no photos of missing children on it, though nowadays many half-gallons do.

"But he was something else," she whispers. "I mean he wanted me to go right up in his hole, you know? And I mean, oh boy."

"Maybe if it's warm tomorrow I can bring water over for a bath," I say. "Do you still have your Caress?"

Natalie says yes but with so little conviction that I'm unsure whether she means it or even understands the question. I do believe she wants to cry, she looks so tortured and weary. "I try to control myself," she says, and I don't think she is talking about her bowels this time. I feel such a deep loneliness in her today, a loneliness not only from her suffering itself but because no one can really understand the nature or intensity of what she goes through moment by moment or day by day. The hopelessness of her existence settles heavily somewhere in my stomach, alongside the queasiness caused by her stench.

"You look beautiful," she tells me then, brightening a bit. "You look like you're dressed up to go, I don't know where. A poetry party?" When I tell her I'm going to the library, Natalie is afraid for me. "Oh, honey," she whispers, "you be careful over there now. You be careful over there. I mean it, too."

"I will," I say. "Don't worry, I will."

When she sees I've brought a plastic bag she starts to gather up several small paper sacks, but then stops and sets them down in front of me. "You do it," she says. "I'm too weak to lift all that up with this side. Beat me up one side and down the other. I quit the goddamn job after he tried to get me up his hole. That's when he set my hair on fire, too."

| | |

Back from the library at 3:15 I see through the window that Natalie is on her feet, fussing and pretending to rearrange the contents of her cart, making very little headway. It looks as if she may be trying to move camp, but within a few minutes I see that she has settled back down into her usual flat position on the sidewalk.

On impulse I decide to offer her water for a bath now, even though my instincts this morning told me this is probably a day to stay away and let her recuperate from last night's battle with the demons. I approach her from behind, another bad idea.

"Would you like to have some water to wash?" I ask, before I notice her angry face.

"Get away from me," she says, low and mean and thick with rage. "You've brought me nothing but trouble, nothing but trouble."

I back away immediately as Natalie mutters and swears, most likely calling me names, though I can't pick up the words and don't want to hear them, anyway. I am as wounded as if she could help herself, even though I know she can't. My feelings are hurt in the most direct and basic of ways, the way one child can be hurt by another. I can't help my pain any more than she can help hers—nothing rational about it. She's an eyesore and a sore on the heart, and I could say she's brought me nothing but trouble, too, but it wouldn't be true.

| | NOVEMBER 22

This morning Natalie is huddled against her cart for shelter from the wind. It got down to 50° during the night, and there is winter in the air, Southern California winter, but winter nonetheless. I won't go over today.

I see the woman with the dog that Natalie often complains about and recognize them from encounters of my own. The woman hands Natalie a small white sack, presumably containing food, while the full-grown German Shepherd sniffs vigorously, first at the sack and then at Natalie herself. She has to turn her back on him before the woman jerks hard enough on his leash to force him down. Even if the animal had no fleas, as Natalie claims he does, it can't be pleasant to have such a large and lively creature sniffing and panting in your face, eyeball to eyeball, as you sit on the ground.

But then I already dislike this woman and this dog, or rather, I dislike this woman, which makes it hard to like the dog because he's so thoroughly hers. Jogging one morning I approached them from behind and took a wide swing into the gutter in order to pass. The dog lunged all the way to the end of his leash and barked at my knee.

"Don't ever run by my dog like that," the woman ordered, angry and no doubt startled.

I stopped to get a look at her. "I beg your pardon?" I said, having heard full well.

"Never run by a dog like that," she said, as if this were a cardinal rule that any idiot should know.

"It's not my fault that you don't train your dog," I said, my hair trigger of urban rage cocked as tight as anyone else's.

"Well, don't run by a dog like that," she repeated firmly, this time as if it were merely the logical conclusion to her flawless argument. This woman is square-shouldered and square-jawed, in her fifties, with violently dyed red hair. She projects an intense myopic squint behind thick lenses and is fond of lecturing young Latinas in the neighborhood on such subjects as littering or teaching their toddlers to cross the street with caution. At least Natalie gets some food in return for putting up with the dog.

| | NOVEMBER 23

After a day apart it's forgive and forget—I forgive, while presumably Natalie forgets that she shooed me away with unkind words. I take her orange juice in a box, a nifty bit of packaging with its own straw attached. As I approach (from the proper side and angle this time), I hear her talking in the whiny, high-pitched voice that was part of the maniacal dialogue the other night. I worry that my presence will agitate her again, but it doesn't seem to.

"How are you, Natalie?" I ask, and the simple question appears to pull her back into ordinary awareness.

"Oh, I'm tired," she says in her usual soft tone, accepting the juice. "I don't know whether I should drink it or not. Have you had yours yet?"

"I just had some," I tell her.

"Well, I'm trying not to eat so much," Natalie says.

"You can save it for another time," I say, pointing out the plastic straw she can use to punch through the box and drink.

"Yes, I know," she says. "The kids are crazy about these things. Marilyn wears big, clear glasses now, but she used to wear dark glasses when I knew her, nearly every time. Marilyn told me to move on down the street, but I did yesterday. I moved all this up that way, and then moved it back up this way." Natalie surveys her belongings and then shrugs, perplexed as to what difference such a move could possibly make. Neither her cart nor any of the bags seem disturbed from their customary arrangement. "But he wants to go up her behind," she assures me. "That's the truth. I hate to say it, but it's the truth." She launches into yet another wild and garbled tale whose central theme, as always, is anal rape.

During the course of this a Black woman from the neighborhood appears and begins to talk to me (not to Natalie, who continues talking as well, raising her voice, in fact, to the level of the competition). Mrs. Atkins has seen a program on TV that gave a number for a homeless women's shelter, and she wants to call and see if she can get Natalie into it.

"Maybe you can talk to her about it," she says, but as she speaks Natalie grows agitated, slapping at random plastic bags and finally escalating into a short but loud and repetitive string of obscenities.

"I don't think she wants to go to a shelter," I tell the woman. "Do you, Natalie? Do you want us to find a place for you to go and live?"

Natalie clams up at this and turns away from us, and I suggest that we move to the corner if we want to talk. Mrs. Atkins seems mystified by what I tell her about Natalie and the paranoia that keeps her from being able to accept shelter. Although she is somewhat aware of the "homeless mentally ill" as a group, the actuality defies her logic.

"You mean she would actually prefer to stay out here on the street? Too many things can happen to her out here. And now cold weather is coming on. Can't we just get somebody to come and pick her up? I do hear her cursing sometimes."

Natalie has been peering around the side of her cart and talking at us, not yelling, but keeping my attention through the whole exchange. I explain quietly that no one can be hospitalized unless directly homicidal or suicidal, or so "gravely disabled" as to be in imminent danger of harm.

"No one I've spoken to so far would consider Natalie's case a priority," I tell Mrs. Atkins. "I work in a facility for homeless mentally ill people, but Natalie is too sick right now to be admitted there. She'd have to give up her cart and bags, agree to bathe and wear clean clothes, share a room with two other women, cooperate in doing chores, and consent to taking anti-psychotic medication. She's not about to do any of that voluntarily without prior treatment."

"What can we do, then?" Mrs. Atkins says. "I think about her out here sometimes. I give her money. I guess we just have to give her what we can when we have it to spare." A car pulls up alongside us, and Mrs. Atkins gets in with her daughter, shaking her head in defeat. I remember her now, this dark and vibrant, impeccably groomed woman in her fifties. When Natalie first appeared in the neighborhood, when she could still maintain the appearance of efficiency on the move, I would see Mrs. Atkins from my window, approaching from way up the street and digging deep into her purse, extracting money and thrusting it into Natalie's hand as she passed. That kind of clear, open willingness to give without being asked is rare now, when so many are asking, day after day.

Natalie is still peering and muttering, calling my name with whispered urgency. I go back, not wanting her to add my conversation with Mrs. Atkins to her wealth of paranoid fantasies. I recount what we were discussing. "We're worried about you out here on the street," I say. "We want to find you a good place to go where you can be safe and see a doctor and get some medicine."

"That's what happened when I worked at General Hospital," Natalie says. "Negroes are trying to undermine everything. You can't ever tell what they'll do, Ann. I'm better off in the fresh air, I know that much. All they do is beat on you in these shelters."

"Well, we were just saying we worry about you, that's all, Natalie. If you got some medication you might not be so frightened all the time. Don't you think that would be a good idea? You said you used to get those shots."

"Sure, and he pulled a gun on me, too. He slit my throat and then he pushed me into the back seat of a car and pulled a gun on me. I had to carry a gun when I was working at Zody's. You know Flossie, don't you, over here at St. Valentine's? Well, she would try to steal everything. Somebody would pay her to do it. I showed you those beads. Well, she took those beads and anything else she could get her hands on. Took my white gloves. They always want money. It's the men, honey, you know that. It's always the men, once you find out."

I am properly overwhelmed and say I have to go.

"Well, okay, then," Natalie says amiably. "Thank you for the juice. Thank you very much."

I ask if she wants me to take the sack beside her and she gives it to me, though she would prefer, as usual, that it were more full before she lets it go. She watches closely and with some distaste as I pull a plastic bag from my pocket, slip it over the sack, and tie it tight. Bags are of primary importance, and I've become obsessed with them myself, even stealing a bunch off a furniture store doorknob the other day—ten or fifteen *brand new bags,* advertising a local outdoor swapmeet. I've taken to carrying the things folded up and concealed about my person now, out of sight until Natalie agrees to let me dispose of something. So far her only protests have been looks of bewilderment and disgust.

Back upstairs I see from the window that she is drinking the juice but not with the straw—instead she turns it straight up and leans her head all the way back, trying to suck from the tiny hole.

Someone has given Natalie a bright pink, quilted nylon bathrobe. A bizarre item, but I suppose nearly everyone has the impulse to give something in the face of powerlessness to do much else.

| | NOVEMBER 24

I take eggs and corn muffins around 11:00. The day is clear, the sun is hot, flies are abuzz, and Natalie is sweating profusely.

"I got up awhile ago and took a little walk, but I had to sit down." She sighs as if the walk were too much for her. I don't believe she's been anywhere, but I do believe she's exhausted. "I didn't get any sleep," she adds. "You got to watch these people around here all the time." I am happy to see that someone has provided her with a fresh gallon of Sparkletts water.

"Did that woman give you a hard time yesterday?" Natalie asks, her tone insinuating she knows this must be true, that she and I, as friends, must have enemies in common.

"She wasn't giving anybody a hard time," I say. "We were just talking about how nice it would be if you had a place to stay with a bed and food and a bathroom to use. You know what I mean?"

"That's Jimmy," Natalie replies, not missing a beat. "He blames me for the death of his mother. Although I didn't have anything to do with it. I was serving the Host, you know, at lunchtime with wafers, and she said *serve me, serve me.* Well, I couldn't just do it all at once like that. And you know what he wanted. This is your body. That's what I told my daughter."

"I didn't know you had a daughter," I say. Somehow this is the most astonishing thing I've ever heard Natalie say, but I believe it, I believe she has a daughter. All this time I have thought of Natalie only as a daughter herself, and now I have to think of her pregnant and giving birth and raising a little girl. Or not raising her. Somewhere in the world is a woman whose mother is Natalie.

"Little Kathy Marie," she says. "But he raped her, too. Stuck his penis right in her mouth and then down between her tiny lips. I tried to scare him off."

I feel a need not to hear this. "Did you know Thanksgiving is day after tomorrow?" I ask.

"I thought it was already past," Natalie says. "Is this the 28th?"

"This is the 24th, and the 26th is Thanksgiving. Day after to-morrow."

"Well, that's what I say. He took that knife and sliced off three slices of turkey, and then he slit my throat with it. He flipped on me. Later on he apologized, but I can't be around the two of them together. He likes it like this, you know," she says, making a fist. "In his hole. And the two of them are awfully fond of each other."

"If it's a nice day on Thanksgiving," I say, "how about if I bring a bucket of water and a cloth. Would you like to wash?"

"Yes, that would be good," Natalie says, surprising me. "But I have to be careful. I was going to change tops last night but it got so cold. I have to be careful of exposing myself, you know."

"Do you still have that bar of Caress?"

"Oh, yes, I still have it," Natalie says. "I used some of that this morning."

I find this difficult to believe, since her face is streaked with grime, but she insists it's true.

"Is that a new sweater you have on?" she asks, which in fact it is. "You don't have any necklace or anything around your neck with it, do you honey?"

I say no, but that I have earrings, and I lean forward to show them off.

"Excuse me, I can't see," she says, and reaches over to push back my hair so she can look. With effort I hold steady, determined not to flinch in the face of this tender gesture, though her gloves and bare fingertips are grievously foul, the dirt not quite obscuring intermittent traces of deep red nail polish.

"Hmmmm," Natalie says, and I see that she'd prefer something a bit more flashy than flat Mexican silver, finely etched.

"You know, when it's your own son that came out of you," she continues, "it makes you want to serve. I just went straight into that cafe and sat right down. A sandwich was three-eighty-nine at that time. When I'd go to the store, he'd accuse me of not having any money. So I went in and gave him my money, seven dollars, and I said, 'You say I don't have no money when I come in here, so you hold this money until I get what I want, and then I'll pay for it.' But that sumbitch, he took my money and wouldn't give it back."

I don't believe there's a son but don't want to ask, either, at least not today. I hand over the paper sack I've brought, which focuses Natalie's attention on the plastic bag beside her.

"Well, the flies are pretty bad around that one," she observes, which I read as permission to remove it. I cross over and pull out the plastic bag I've stashed in my pocket and quickly slip hers inside it. I can feel her responding to this, to my having that secret bag, but all she says, forlornly, is, "I wish you had used this one, really," wanting me to use the paper as always and leave the plastic for her.

| | NOVEMBER 25

It is 40° at 6:30 a.m., and Natalie is using the same covering as when it's 70°, though her cart displays at least three blankets and bedspreads piled in easy reach. I stop by with another box of orange juice on my way to work, which seems to cheer her. She has one glove off, a rare occurrence, and is picking at her fingernails. In her lap is the bar of Caress in its pink box, somewhat worn but still intact.

"You have the soap, Natalie. That's very good."

"Yes," she says, proud of herself. "I noticed that the ends of my fingers were a little bit dirty." She drops this information casually, as if she were otherwise immaculate, and for a moment I wonder if she sensed my stiffening at her touch yesterday.

"Well, hold onto that Caress," I say. "Tomorrow I'll bring a bucket of nice warm water."

"Okay," Natalie says. "I'm ready for it."

"You've got your lipstick on," I say. "You look pretty this morning."

"Well, I thank you," she beams. "My lips were a wee bit dry, you know, from this cold air."

As I drive off she is struggling to open the juice box, refusing again to utilize the straw.

Crawling through traffic I get carried away with the idea that I might find Natalie a new skirt and actually convince her to wash and put on clean underwear and socks and change skirts, if not tops. An agency near work distributes food and clothing to the homeless, at least to the homeless who can find transportation to the office, prove themselves sober, submit to an in-depth interview, and fill out an application. We sometimes send our clients over there when we run low on clothes, and the agency gratefully refers their "disturbed" cases to us, pronto.

At the admittance desk I run smack into a bureaucratic wall in the form of a long and lean, balding, sixtyish man in dark glasses who tells me curtly in a thick German accent that they are not giving out clothes today. When I exert a touch of neighborly pressure, he decides I need a voucher, that I have to get somebody official from next door to sign it, that he can't lend me his pen to fill out the form, and that he will have to go into the back room with me to see who's there and whether I can be admitted, even if I get the voucher okayed. They are not giving out clothing today, he says, *because they have too much clothing piled up.* I search his face in vain for some hint of irony.

"It's the day before Thanksgiving," I say finally, as calmly as I can manage. "Can't I just duck back there and grab some kind of skirt for a bag lady? Does it have to be so complicated?"

"It *iss* the day before Thanksgiving," he says crisply. "Vich iss vy ve are giffink turkeys."

"She doesn't need a turkey," I say. "She doesn't have a stove. All she needs is a damn skirt."

"I vassn't sayink she could haff a turkey. She vould haff to come in herself."

I loathe this man for reminding me of the stereotypical *Nazi.* His job can't be an easy one. But I bet if I make a scene he will take it out on future clients we send over. I wad up the blank voucher and toss it into his wastebasket and manage not to use any ugly language when I tell him never mind, that I wouldn't think of putting him to so much extra trouble.

"Happy Thanksgiving," I say at the door.

"You haff a nice day," he answers back.

I get to work late with a whopping headache. From the back of our women's closet I dig out a skirt that might fit Natalie, not ideal, but below the knee at least. At lunchtime I travel to a nearby thrift shop, hoping for a better find. The shop is closed with no indication why—according to the schedule it should be open. Closed for the holiday, maybe, right when it ought to be open extra. I peer inside and pound hard on the door, knowing this is futile. I pound and pound until my hand starts to ache and I become conscious of the knot of anger that resides in my belly—about Natalie and all of it.

ǀ ǀ THANKSGIVING DAY

I stop to check on her as I come back from my run. It is a brisk, clear morning, down to 45° during the night but pleasantly warm now if you're active or in the sun.

"How are you, Natalie?" I ask.

"How are you, how are you," she answers sarcastically. "How do you think I am?"

"I don't know," I say evenly. "How are you?"

She calms down visibly. She was talking to herself when I approached, and a man and little boy had just passed by. I think it took her a moment to realize who I was and switch into talking to me.

"He came over here talking up high like this," she says in a whispered screech. "I-EE-I-EE! And he said I talk too low. I said I can't help it if I talk like a man, you know. I can't help what comes out of my throat." She rubs her throat as if she may have strained her voice.

"Have you had any coffee today?" I ask, and she shakes her head emphatically no.

"I don't know whether I want any or not," she says. "I like to have a big cup of coffee in the morning, but they can't understand that. Why do you want a big one? Why this and why that. They don't have any idea what it's like to be out...."

She stops mid-sentence, but I am almost certain she was about to say they don't have any idea what it's like to be out on the street. This would have been the first objective reference I ever heard Natalie make to her status or condition, and she couldn't quite complete it out loud.

"Will you feel like washing if I bring a bucket over later?" I ask, but she is in her stubborn, defiant mood.

"I don't feel like doing anything," she says, emphasizing each word separately.

"Well, I'll check with you later," I say, backing away. She waits until I am nearly to the corner.

"A cup of coffee might be nice," she calls out. "Do you need money to go get it?"

"It's homemade," I tell her. "Don't worry about it."

| | |

When I return with coffee, Natalie has a small plastic sandwich bag full of quarters, which she quickly shoves deep into another sack under trash.

"Happy Thanksgiving," I say.

"Happy Thanksgiving to you, too," she replies, having switched in my absence from nasty to sweet. "Where's yours? Don't you drink any coffee yourself? You must have already swallowed the whole thing to start with, huh?"

"Maybe somebody will bring you a bite of turkey today," I say. "I would if I were cooking. But I can bring soup if you don't get something else."

Natalie whispers a few garbled sentences that seem to indicate she has twenty dollars in her bra. "I can reach in there anytime, if I can reach it," she says. I see that she has twenty-one cents in her open palm, and I suggest that I might buy her some bananas with it when I go to the store later on, but Natalie changes the subject in her expert way. Her offers to pay for things are merely gestures that belie the need to hoard her cash. Passersby, guilty in the land of plenty, are giving her money because it's Thanksgiving, but she may have accumulated quite a sum, anyway, over the weeks, since she never spends anything. I think it would be good if she gave me some token in exchange for what I bring—good for her, I mean, as well as helping me with the money. I'm reluctant to broach this subject, though—very touchy business, I can tell—high on the paranoia scale. She is full of stories about people stealing her money, and of course, some of them are bound to be true.

As I sit on the sidewalk listening to her ramble, I begin to feel pessimistic about the skirt I brought home and even about the bath itself. The skirt is more or less a straight skirt, and I see that what Natalie needs is exactly what she has—a long skirt, wide at the bottom for ease in sitting and lying down and sleeping, as well as for convenience in squatting and remaining covered and keeping the cloth away from the mess as she goes to the bathroom. She will never take off that top or that jacket because she's got too much stuff stored in there—and a bra full of booty as well. Today she has two or three extra blackened wooden clothespins clamped around the waistband of her skirt for a better fit. This must be very uncomfortable, digging into her belly and side—obviously Natalie isn't too sensitive to discomfort.

"Are you listening to me? Are you listening to me? Are you listening to me?" she is saying.

"Yes," I say. "I am."

"Are you? Are you listening? If you can hear what I even mean." She leans over toward me and motions for me to lean closer and closer until for a second I think she is going to kiss me, but she whispers instead, right in my ear. I can hardly make out a word.

"You're talking a blue streak," I tell her, pulling back. "I can't keep up with you today. How about if I bring some water? Look what a gorgeous day we have."

"Don't change clothes right out in the yard," Natalie warns (either me or herself). "He said, don't you have better sense than to take your clothes off right out in the yard? Why don't you go inside? Don't you have the dignity to go inside?"

"I understand that," I tell her. "But the point is, you don't have any inside to go to right now. So can't we just do the best we can if I bring out some water?" Natalie won't consent, so I say I'll check back later.

"He'll hit you over the head," she says as I start away. "Hit you in the heart, hit you in the gut, bend over and go up your ass, cut you with that pocket knife, put that up your ass and cut you down below."

"Do you still remember my name?" I ask. "I bet you've forgotten my name by now, haven't you?"

"I remember your name," Natalie says, but I sense she is bluffing.

"Ann," I say.

"That's right. Ann. Ann? That's right. Ann. But you remind me of a woman on television. Boy, I mean they got after her, too. They didn't like to take orders from a woman, you know, and they just beat her till I don't know what. But then she hauled off and kicked that one right between the legs." Natalie starts to laugh uproariously and I join in, a laugh on her terms, which I don't entirely understand, but a laugh together, nonetheless. "Just about did him in," she concludes proudly. "Just about did the sumbitch in."

"Good for her," I say. "That's the way to go, don't you think?"

Upstairs after a while I see an Asian woman who often feeds Natalie hand her a covered bowl. In a neighborhood so heavily populated with Asians and Latinos the chances of her getting traditional turkey with trimmings are slim. I wish I had thought to buy a frozen dinner, but it's too late now—the freezer at the Mexican market has been on the blink for weeks.

| | |

Around 12:30 I decide to risk taking a bucket of water, a washcloth, a plastic bag, a pair of warm knee socks, and a pair of cotton underpants. Natalie is busy drinking a diet Coke.

"I don't feel like bathing right now," she says, petulant lady of leisure that she is.

"Well, I'm here now," I point out. "Better give it a try while you have the chance. Baths don't grow on trees, you know." This seems to startle us both into laughing, and I wonder if she is seeing in her mind what I am seeing in mine—miniature bathtubs festooning the palm fronds above us. She drains the last of her soda and aims the can toward her cart with a casual toss, ignoring its rebound to the sidewalk where it's blown by a breeze into the street. With effort she rises to her feet and begins to fish among the mysteries in her sea of bags, still chuckling, until she comes up with the bar of pink soap, unboxed now and smeared with grime.

I wet the washcloth for her, and she scrubs vigorously at her face and neck, jabbering nonstop and neglecting to use soap. The cloth grows blacker and blacker until suddenly she drops it into the bucket with a hearty splash. "I don't use soap on my face," she states, as if I had asked. With an air of defiance she removes both her gloves and sets them carefully in the center of her furry bed. "He told me not to take our gloves off," she says, apparently shocked by her own action. "We don't usually take our gloves off."

I am reluctant to say a word, afraid of distracting her and breaking this pleasantly surprising momentum. She takes off what's left of the knee-high hose I gave her weeks ago, now badly tattered as well as filthy. "He'll be over here to turn the whole damn cart over tonight," she mutters. "You wait and see if he doesn't." As if to emphasize the drama of this, Natalie grabs onto the handle of the cart and sticks first one then the other leg into the bucket. She performs this alternate soaking several times before she gets around to using the soap and washcloth on both legs together, ankle to mid-thigh. Then without hesitation she hikes up her skirt and pulls off her double pair of soiled panties while I get the plastic bag open and ready for quick deposit. Up under the skirt, with concentrated effort, she washes her private parts, even as people pass by on the sidewalk across the street or drive to the corner stop sign and stare. I try to stand between them and Natalie as best I can, keeping my back to her all the while and spreading my arms, as if this might help.

"And when I kissed her, she came," Natalie whispers, scrubbing away. I can feel her looking at me, but I don't look back. "She was up on the bed, you know, but the odor was terrible. I'm telling you, I had to leave the room that odor was so bad. What are you thinking about, Ann?"

I am thinking how horrid it must feel not to keep yourself clean. "I'm just thinking what a beautiful day it is," I tell her. "I'm glad you're taking this chance to freshen up a little bit. Aren't you?" This sets her to muttering again about "him" and "his" threats, how everything she has achieved so far (taking off gloves, undressing in public, washing with soap) is strictly forbidden by "him."

"They don't want Nattie to take any of the pleasure," she says. "Just get up, get to the dance, bend at the waist, and you know what."

"The hell with all of them," I say. "You can keep that washcloth if you like."

"Don't you need it?" Natalie says, but she's already about to stick it into a bag.

"Rinse it out and let it dry first," I tell her. "Maybe you can use it again." She complies for once, draping the rag (for now it is a rag) halfway across the handle of her cart.

The dark blue knee socks I've brought seem to please her, not only for their color and fit but because the side of each sock has a small pocket sewn in. "You can hide stuff in there if you like," I point out, which I'm sure Natalie is figuring, too. She eyes me suspiciously, though, as if I know too much now and may betray her.

"I can't wear men's socks," she says, pulling at them as if to tear them off. "It doesn't do to put on a man's sock. He'll have it into a bloody pulp that won't quit. I told you that much. Bombarding everything."

"They're not men's socks, Natalie. They're my own socks. They're girl-socks. I used to wear them all the time. They're too small for a man's foot. Keep them on. They'll be nice and warm, and besides, they match your skirt." I distract her with the underwear, plain beige cotton, which she does deign to pull on, even as she registers a low, buzzing complaint about their lack of lace.

"Now let me see you," I say. She looks brighter and smells almost decent, though the socks are the major difference that a stranger would notice. "Very chipper," I tell her. "Now that blue cap can bring out the blue in your eyes. I'm going to find you another skirt one of these days, too. You look like a new woman, Natalie. Quite lovely."

"I guess they'll turn the whole damn cart over," she says, but she is smiling from the compliments. "What else can I do? They want to rot your face off as it is."

"Maybe you can wash out your gloves before I empty the bucket," I say.

"Oh, we don't wash our gloves," Natalie says, but she stoops to pick them up.

"They're cotton or nylon, aren't they?" I ask. "It'll be all right to wash them."

"Do you wash your gloves? We don't wash our gloves, I don't think."

"I wash mine all the time," I assure her. "I think it's good for them, actually."

Natalie drops the gloves suddenly into the murky water, then acts as if she has surprised herself again. "Better let them soak," she says, straightening her cap. "They're silk, you know. Solid silk in a springtime hue."

I hadn't counted on waiting for a soak.

"What do you think about everything?" Natalie asks. "Why don't you talk?"

"Well, really," I say, "I'm thinking that if you have to take a bath on the street, you have a beautiful day to do it. So that is something to be thankful for, I guess, if we want to make a list of what we're thankful for."

"Yes, it's windy at times, though," Natalie says. "I shouldn't have taken off those hose, because it made my feet too cold."

"But now you have warm socks instead," I say.

"I don't like to mention it," she whispers, looking past me as if there is someone behind. "If you tell it, they'll rip out each compartment until they find what they want."

"You don't have to hide anything in the socks," I say. "Nobody's going to know the difference."

"That's what you think," Natalie says, stooping over to slosh the gloves around in the bucket. "I'm the one they'll slambang with that pipe."

The gloves have left the water inky black, and Natalie hangs them to dry with the washcloth. She sniffs her fingertips and smiles. "There's a cream in it," she says. "Twenty-mule-team Borax."

"Don't you feel better?" I ask her. "I feel better, and I'm not even the one who had the bath."

"Do you really, Ann?"

"Yes, I do," I say. "I think we got a lot accomplished."

"It's too much work for you," Natalie says. "You can't be careful enough, really." She lowers herself slowly to her knees on the fur coat lining, then tumbles sideways so she can sit.

"I'm going to the store," I say, "if you want anything."

Natalie reaches down into a sack and pulls out the soiled plastic sandwich bag full of quarters, rambling again about people stealing from her.

"If you gave me two of those quarters," I say, "I could get you fifty cents worth of bananas."

"I had two quarters somewhere," she says. I make no comment on the twenty or twenty-five quarters she has in her hand. "I had seven. So this is six dollars and forty cents." She reaches back below again and pulls up another filthy sandwich bag, which does indeed contain two quarters. "Usually I better just tell you what I want and you tell me how much it was, then."

"If you give me fifty cents," I repeat, "I could get you fifty cents worth of bananas, however many that might be."

In slow motion, the way she sometimes surrenders feces, Natalie hands me over the two-quarter bag.

"Just bananas?" I ask. "Anything else?"

"No. You get whatever you want to get. You're the one with the money."

At home I find her a new sandwich bag, the kind that seals, and at the store I get forty-nine cents worth of bananas. I put her receipt and a penny into the new bag and take her the bananas, plus an orange I bought. The fruits are in separate plastic bags, and I let Natalie keep these and the large bag containing both of them, plus one of the swap-meet bags I stole. All this plastic seems to make her genuinely happy—I think I've made her Thanksgiving at last.

"I had $173 for you at one time, Ann," she tells me cheerily as I take leave. "But they beat me up and took it all." She studies the receipt as if it holds a secret.

| | |

Soaking in the tub I toy with the idea of staying home and cooking for Natalie and me rather than dressing up and driving to Venice for dinner. It will be a large gathering, and I'm sure I wouldn't be missed. Still, it would be ungracious to renege on the invitation. Besides, staying here might seem too strange or weird. Unhealthy, even. Downright eccentric. It might dawn on me that I'm not spending this holiday the way one is supposed to, though of course you're not really supposed to spend it, either, among people who wouldn't miss you if you weren't there. I ought to be lonely and depressed, but at the moment I'm too exhilarated over Natalie—somewhat clean, somewhat content, even somewhat a participant in the great American Thanksgiving economy. Be still my poor, Puritanical, capitalistic heart.

| | NOVEMBER 27

I take eggs over around noon, realizing as I cross the street that I've forgotten to bring a bag along. Natalie's clear plastic cover is disarranged over her bags, and there is another plastic cover over

NATALIE ON THE STREET |

her cart, a new development since yesterday. Last night was quite cold, down to the middle forties with gusty winds.

"I was just reminiscing about being over there on Hoover, you know," Natalie says, sitting up as I approach. "They had that baby in the back seat of that car, and, I don't like to say anything, but they were strangling that baby and tried to make out like I did it. I told them not to hold that baby so tight around its neck. I shouldn't say it, but he took that baby's life. He took that baby's life."

I ask if she was cold last night, but Natalie won't admit to it.

"I'm just sore from having that water on me," she says.

I mention twice that I have eggs, but she does not reach out to accept them. The third time she says to put them in the nearest bag, which I do. It's a bad sign when she won't take what I bring in her own hands and hold it or put it away herself. She pulls the small plastic bag with yesterday's bananas from underneath her blanket. Two of them are missing.

"See where they came off at the stalk?" Natalie says accusingly. "I took them and blessed them, but now that's the way they are."

"Do you have any garbage for me to take?" I ask.

Natalie picks up an aluminum pan full of diarrhea which, covered with Saran Wrap, looks exactly like an uncooked pumpkin pie.

"You have to put it in something," I tell her. "I can't carry it like that."

"Go get a brown bag, then," Natalie snaps, the first direct order, or even request, that I've ever heard her utter.

I bring back a double paper bag in a plastic bag for the mess, plus a spare for Natalie to keep. As I hold open the double sack, she spills the pie pan into it and throws in a couple of mushy banana peels for good measure. I think if I let myself breathe in I might throw up before I can get the paper bag sealed inside the white plastic one. As I start this maneuver, though, Natalie becomes agitated.

"DON'T PUT THAT IN THE WHITE BAG!" she shouts. "WE DON'T HAVE TO LET EVERYBODY KNOW OUR PERSONAL BUSINESS!"

"I have to put it in here to take it, Natalie. Just keep your hands off it."

Quick and nimble, Natalie rises to her feet, reaches beneath her blanket, and pulls out a shockingly long piece of black metal pipe.

"I WILL NOT BE WITHOUT FOOD, ANN," she says, trembling with anger—or fear. "DIDN'T I TELL YOU I HAD TO BEAT HER HALFWAY TO DEATH WHEN SHE TRIED TO FIND OUT WHAT I HAD IN THESE SOCKS?"

This fit has come on so suddenly that I am more than slightly shaken. "There's no food in this bag, honey," I say, but Natalie raises the pipe to strike and yells something I can't make out. I jump away quickly and walk straight across the street with no backward glance, which shuts her up.

I do believe she'd have hit me. After all her stories of being beaten with a pipe, she turns out to have one all her own. I will stay away for a while. The woman is burdensome at her best, unbearable at her worst.

| | |

Once my knees stop trembling, I wonder why such deterioration since yesterday? The more paranoid people get, the more likely they are to become irrationally aggressive (when everything and everyone appear to be a threat, you defend yourself by attacking). For a moment I fantasize about Natalie being picked up and hospitalized as "homicidal." I could stretch the truth a bit. She might get cleaned up, at least, and fed, and maybe put on medication that would improve her thinking enough that she could manage better for herself, or even go to a board-and-care. The heavy weight of the mental health system stops me from continuing this line of thought, especially since Natalie is so adamant about refusing help.

Yesterday may have been too much of an intrusion for her—the bath, the underwear and complicated socks, the money transaction, all the holiday visitors and helpers, donations and passersby. In addition to the usual craziness over bags, it may be that Natalie got confused and thought I was taking one of her bags with bananas or other food in it. Then, too, I was a bit brusque and impatient with her this morning, not listening long enough to soothe her, unwilling to linger and coax because of the stench. It was difficult to conceal my displeasure and frustration at the mess, just one day after the hard-won bath. The bath made her "sore," and I'm sore, too, drained from the rush of adrenalin that came with the threat of attack.

If it were simple, if I could simply call what used to be referred to as "the men in the white coats," I suppose I would gather all my nerve and do it.

I am in definite need of a break and have vowed not to look out the window today. The temperature dropped to the mid-forties again last night, and I piled on quilts enough to bend back my toes. One of these years I'll give in and buy myself an electric heater with a thermostat. One of these trips to the laundromat my ancient covers will finally fall apart, and I'll cough up the money for a heater, justifying it as necessity rather than luxury. No need for extravagance when you can make do without. I try to view this stubborn stingy streak in myself as a virtue, not always an easy task. The solitary life allows austerity to flourish. *Cough up the money. Make do.* Money as phlegm, money as shit. Natalie tries to hold onto both her money and her shit. I keep suggesting that she put some distance between herself and her camp when she has to go to the bathroom (a euphemism that in itself excludes her). So far, at least so far as I can tell, she refuses to walk up the street to do her business. *Don't foul your own nest*—there's one proverb she'd do well to take literally, as schizophrenics are famous for doing. The only other sensible solution is to keep on moving the nest itself—shit and move on, like birds on the wing, or dogs on the leash.

At Thanksgiving dinner in Venice there were three fashionably large dogs present among the company of twenty or thirty people, and the owner of one, a television actress, became concerned that her animal had overeaten and would probably suffer an upset stomach—too much turkey white meat and cornbread dressing and beets and cranberry sauce. I know I wouldn't have found this so offensive if I'd been among people I knew well and cared for, but it turned out I knew almost no one except the host. I did have an interesting conversation with a cinematographer—we discovered there's a certain Kirk Douglas-Kim Novak movie we both watch year after year whenever it comes on TV, the one where he's a married architect and she's an intriguingly sexy, disenchanted housewife. We almost couldn't think of the name of the film but finally remembered: *Strangers When We Meet*. I started to get a headache from the nonalcoholic cabernet and from not knowing anyone and from the idea of dogs eating what Natalie doesn't have. My friend would have been more than happy to provide a "doggie bag" for Natalie, but under the circumstances I lacked the energy to explain.

| | |

Pulling quilts from the closet shelf, I discovered that in the flannel-backed wool one my mother made there are squares from a green and brown plaid skirt I wore in elementary school in the early fifties. I can remember how its hem scratched the back of my knees just above where my socks left off, below my cotton slip. Winter coats came with heavy leggings then, double lined for the walk to school in snow and bitter wind. I went to Horace Mann and was proud, except I thought kids who went to Mark Twain or Thomas Jefferson had the better deal because nobody knew who Horace Mann was. In fifth grade I got on a biography kick—the tiny library offered one whole shelf of turquoise hardbacks with the names of their subjects written in deep red script on the front. Horace Mann didn't have his own volume, but I was excited to find his name in *Dorothea Dix*. For a long time I thought of Horace Mann as a famous teacher who helped Dorothea Dix establish insane asylums. Apparently she believed that if the mentally ill were given shelter and decent food and kind treatment, their unfortunate symptoms would abate. If she was ignorant, at least she was humanely ignorant.

There was an "insane asylum" less than a mile from where we lived, which my family referred to formally as the State Hospital, informally as Out on the Hill ("Quit acting like you belong Out on the Hill"). I wonder now what conditions really existed in that place, which certainly looked welcoming enough from the highway, albeit institutional, with low brick buildings and lots of trees and grass and tillable acreage (hence "funny farm," no doubt). Our house was at the edge of town, across from the train station, at the end of the busline. Buses ran every half hour, but every third one would bypass Lucille Street and continue Out on the Hill to make its turnaround and pick up or deposit passengers, mainly employees, or patients with privileges—*inmates*, I believe they were called. In winter we'd watch out the living room window instead of waiting at the stop. When the bus zoomed on by, we'd have plenty of time to bundle up and get across the street before it came back from the hospital. Sometimes there would be a patient or two on board—thick black shoes, coarse clothing, unkempt hair. If there were no attendant nurse, my mother might cuddle both my hands in hers, or even take me onto her lap. The specter of madness somehow holds more terror for us than all the worst of bodily ills.

I went on to read the blue biographies of Jane Addams and Lucretia Mott and Clara Barton—all those brave and stern, semi-subversive, do-good gals. (We had a school named after Clara Barton, too, but it was the oldest and least kept up in town.)

More and more it seems to me that compassion dwells in the tough, not the tender-hearted, because it requires us to come to terms with our own capacity (or incapacity) for suffering, and it calls for action rather than sentiment. It also requires us to get past the guilt and resentment we feel when we come face to face with someone whose suffering is greater than our own.

On the Venice boardwalk some weeks ago I found myself walking behind a young woman with only one leg who was using a crutch quite skillfully, moving right along. This woman was unusually attractive and, most remarkably, wore a miniskirt, exposing her one long, shapely, graceful leg. As we approached the bike path, another young woman took a curve too fast and skidded into a nasty spill on the concrete. Without hesitation the woman with the crutch rushed to see if she'd been hurt. Even from where I stood I could see two bloody knees, but I could also see the cyclist's face as she realized the plight of her would-be rescuer.

"I'm fine," she kept saying, visibly shaken. "Really, I'm fine." She jumped back onto her bike and rode off with determination, not even taking the usual moment to regain her bearings or composure. Though she, not the amputee, was the one in obvious pain, there seemed to be something instinctively shameful about accepting help or sympathy from one whose suffering appeared both transcendent and permanent. Ironically, the kinder, more gracious response would have been to accept the comfort offered.

I think when we see someone who is genuinely crazy we are similarly shamed by the superficiality of our own day-to-day emotional anguish and confusion and despair and by the depth of self-pity that often accompanies them. It is terrifying to face the "givens" in life, both what we are given and what we are spared. I could be Natalie, she could be me. It's not as if we somehow earned our individual fates.

I had intended to wait another day, at least, but on my way back from running I stop to check on Natalie. I approach delicately, and she greets me pleasantly, calmer than I expected, since she has already been up and moving around this morning. Her cart is five or six feet closer to the corner, and she is in the process of relocating some of her bags.

"How are you?" I ask.

"I'm all right."

"Are you cold? It's not even fifty out here yet."

"I'm not cold now particularly," Natalie says, on her knees and keeping busy with the bags. "Are you cold?"

I am squatting a few feet farther back from her than usual. "Are you still mad at me?" I feel like a child saying this, and I say it in a childlike way. I have debated whether to refer to the incident on Friday, not wanting to risk agitating her again but not wanting to pretend it never happened, either. She seems cooperative and stable enough for me to bring up the subject. "Are you still mad at me, Natalie?"

"I'm not mad at you," she says, almost reassuring, even almost maternal. "I was just hurting so bad. I've tried to cut down on what I eat. That woman brings me rice and things that are so salty. She uses a lot more salt than I would use if I was fixing it for myself, you know. And I don't complain. I don't like to complain. But I'm afraid I've hurt somebody's feelings." Natalie looks at me directly now. "You know, I wanted to wash my hands and comb my hair. I just did that. But they want you to get up and exercise. I did yesterday. I walked and walked. But they come in the night, you know, and they're jealous because of what I have. Yes, the men are jealous and the women are jealous." She keeps looking me in the eye, and her tone is low but very, very intense. There is great feeling behind what she is saying, not like her usual conspiratorial whisper or hollow, angry mutter. "I worked for six years, getting those people up and dressed and getting them to the breakfast table," she says. "I had to tell those Negroes everything that was on their plate. In a place like that, when they say get up, you have to do it right now. Eddie was supposed to take care of the table, but he put that off on me, too." She grabs her abdomen as if in sudden pain.

"Is your stomach hurting you?" I ask.

"Well, it was," Natalie says. "But awhile ago I ate that orange and it went away."

I offer to bring juice and coffee.

"That sounds pretty good," she says. "That would be awfully nice if you have the time."

When I return, the cart has been rolled a few feet closer to the corner, and Natalie is on her feet, fussing over bags and fussing out loud.

"I get so tired of them tormenting me day and night, night and day. Where you gonna go, where you gonna sleep, what you gonna do. Not a minute's peace. You understand what I'm saying? Would you like somebody at you that way all the time?"

"No," I say, "I wouldn't."

"I worked days and nights and overtime, honey. And if I spoke to you brusquely about the bananas, then I'm sorry. But I know seven from six and six from five. Jimmy had that firearm and just kept on strangling that child, and I had to get that gun and shoot it. To protect my heart. Do you understand?" I nod. She is still speaking with real depth of feeling, intensely earnest, and then she puts her hand over her heart. "To protect my heart," she says. "To protect my very own heart. Can you understand that or not?"

"Yes," I say. "I can understand it. We have to protect our hearts."

I offer her the new plastic bag I've brought, and she accepts it gladly, immediately pulling out a clear plastic box that contains a barren turkey leg. She removes the bone and drops it into the new bag, then jerks it right back out and thrusts it at me to look at.

"We don't show that," she says emphatically. "Would you show that? We don't show everything about our personal secrets. But they want to come and pick and pick and pry and pry." She waves the bone about, then drops it into the bag. "Where I used to live it didn't matter where you went, it was dangerous one way and dangerous the other. And to say things about another race, these Central Americans that were let out of these jails have killed more old women and children than you can count. You don't give up what God gives you, Ann." She sounds on the verge of tears as she begins to cross herself again and again. "Can't you understand that?" she pleads. "You don't give up what God gives you."

Something is going on here. I think Natalie may be on the move, but I restrain myself from asking. I don't want to "pick and pry," and I don't want to agitate her, and I don't want to interfere or even distract her. She is full of peculiar energy today, and it will be good if she can use it to abandon some of her own filth and find a fresh spot to camp. Still, it is oddly upsetting to watch her out the window, gathering bags and rearranging first the cart and then the bags, even trying on coats and sweaters and taking them back off, tossing them onto the top of the cart, which is already piled precariously high with layers of blankets over trash. The bright blue plastic cloth I gave her weeks and weeks ago for rain suddenly reappears, draped expansively over the side of the cart.

I feel as if I have received an apology for the attack, Natalie's version of an apology, anyway, or apologia. I was startled to hear her use the word *brusquely*—"I'm sorry if I spoke to you brusquely about the bananas." It's not only an unusual word for her to say, but it's also the word I wrote to describe myself—how *I* spoke to *her* brusquely before she raised the pipe. Everything she said this morning held such poignancy. I think she was touched by my asking if she was still mad at me, by the fact that I cared whether she was or not and said so. It seemed to unlock a stream of feeling in her beyond (or beneath) the omnipresent paranoia. I have wept for her before today but never in her presence. If she realized, she gave no sign.

| | |

When I return from the store just past noon, there is a cop car parked at Natalie's corner, two officers sitting inside and watching her pack in her inimitable fashion. So someone did finally call the police, most likely the people in the yellow frame house right alongside her camp. Who can blame them after these many weeks of tolerance? The last time I estimated the number of Natalie's bags it looked like ten or twelve. Now, as she gathers them all around where she stands, I think there must be twenty or more. After a while the officers back up and turn around in the intersection and then park beneath my window to continue their surveillance.

With some gleaning of nerve I go down to find out what they have to say, if anything, about Natalie's situation. We chat for a bit, both of them friendly and pleasant Caucasian men, about the way she's been living. "Now that you're called in," I say, "is there any chance you could get this woman into a hospital?"

"Absolutely none whatsoever," the younger one says. "I am amazed, but there is absolutely nothing we can do in a case like this except respond to complaints and make the person move on."

"If she was in a back alley, it wouldn't be so bad," the older one adds. "But right here on the corner, at an intersection, so close to people's yards? No way, José."

I think it would be much worse if Natalie were in an alley, but I tamp down indignation and keep this to myself. Why can't there be one person whose fault this all is, so I can grab him by the lapels and demand he set things right at once? Not bad duty for these guys on a Sunday afternoon, sitting snug and warm in an official car, supervising the eviction of a crazy old woman who holds no lease on anything at all. They intend to linger until Natalie is completely clear of the corner property, indeed the source of the complaint.

"You may have quite a wait," I tell them, pointing out how Natalie has to move the cart a few steps at a time, then pick up her twenty-plus bags two or three at a time and haul them forward to the cart, then fuss with the whole arrangement before she shoves the cart again. My tone implies—I know it does but can't seem to help it—that there might be other, better ways for the L.A.P.D. to serve and protect these gang-ridden streets. By the time I get upstairs their car is gone and I feel shaken, uncertain whether I'm proud or ashamed of myself. Any encounter with uniformed authority must inspire some guilt.

Perhaps the woman from the corner house has seen them leave, for she has come out onto her porch with a broom, shooing Natalie away in Spanish. "Vamos!" she calls. "Vamos, vamos, vamos!" This tiny, thick-waisted woman has had it now, has put up with Natalie long enough and is determined to sweep her out of sight, is even willing to stand in the yard and halfway threaten her with the broom. Natalie, however, is taking her sweet time, occasionally shouting back, although I can't catch her words. At one point she drops the bag she is transferring and stomps into the yard to shake her fist at the woman, retreating abruptly when a small child appears on the porch.

"Go, go, go," the woman yells in English. "Farther, farther, farther."

The child, not long out of diapers, hops into the fray as well. "Go, go! Go, go, go!" he calls as he climbs down the steps. An annoying little black and brown and white terrier is running about the yard yapping at Natalie, too, finally trotting up to piss on one of her bags when her back is turned. Everybody's as territorial as hell all of a sudden, and it would be comical if it weren't so painful to watch.

Under the guise of tidying up her porch and yard the señora remains outside to keep an eye on Natalie, who by now has managed to move her entire camp from the side of the house to smack dab in front of it. The woman is determined that Natalie not settle there, where she would be even more disruptive than before. Each time Natalie takes a breather from her efforts the woman waves her arms in a broad "vamoose" gesture. Soon she connects a hose and begins to wash and sweep along the sidewalk where Natalie used to live. The two of them keep exchanging hostile looks, and I think the woman must feel tempted to hose Natalie down as well. The number of bags and the amount of stuff in and around them appears even greater than awhile ago—additional inventory seems to have materialized from nowhere, as if Natalie's belongings somehow doubled once she started poking around in them.

I am concerned because I can see that Natalie isn't feeling well—she keeps holding her stomach as if in pain, and she has to keep stopping to rest. I want to go grab the cart and push it way up the street for her and then help her carry the bags, but I resist this impulse, thinking it will be better if she can do it alone. I don't want to add to the agitation or associate myself in her mind with the eviction. I hope she didn't see me talking with the cops, either.

Eventually, after relentless barking from the dog and goading from the woman, Natalie manages a rage-filled, herculean push that lands the cart two whole houses farther up the street. She has to make many, many trips back down the hill for bags then, a slow and arduous process, especially since most of the time she is using one hand to clutch at her waist (either in pain or to hold up her skirt). At last everything is transported up to where the cart is except for one large piece of plastic, which Natalie must be too exhausted to retrieve. The señora waters everywhere now, everywhere Natalie has been this day, wetting the sheet of plastic, too, though she keeps trying to kick it to the gutter. Up the street Natalie stands and observes this rite of purification, leaning on her cart, shaking an occasional fist, ultimately shouting about the FBI. Then suddenly she stoops over, in pain I think at first, but apparently she is peeing into a container of some kind under her skirt. She throws the urine onto the grass beside where she is standing among all the bags, which extend at least ten feet behind the cart. She has the sidewalk completely blocked alongside a hedge, right at the entrance to a two-story apartment building. Natalie spreads out her furry coat lining and sits down carefully. Most likely that's as far as she will get today, though I can't believe she'll be tolerated long there, so highly visible to everyone entering and leaving that address. They'll be forced to walk around her and smell what there is to smell. The woman who called the police has gathered up her broom and her dog and her grandchild now and has closed her door with emphasis. Unless you are facing the sun, the air has grown uncomfortably cool, and I fasten my north windows tight against the breeze.

| | |

As the afternoon wears on Natalie calms herself, fussing over her arrangement of bags, settling in like any new tenant, kneeling for a while, then sitting, then standing again to lean on the cart, hand on hip, surveying the angle of installation and the novelty of a hillside vantage point. I decide to see how she is, and on the way I pick up the large double plastic sheet, which looks like it once held a new mattress. It is still wet, but I drag it along anyway, and Natalie seems grateful. She greets me first, which is unusual, like maybe I'm a friend from the old neighborhood.

"You must be tired," I say, "after all that work. You've had quite a busy day today."

"You better believe it," Natalie says. "Moving is one thing that'll wear you out. I had sweat pouring all over this body."

"You don't realize how much stuff you have until you start to move," I say. This is what everyone says who moves, and it has to be said for Natalie, too.

"Seems like it's a lot of hard work to wear you out with or something. I don't know. I think that woman was jealous when other people gave me things. And that blanket. She was mad because she gave it to me and it got so dirty. Well, I can't help it if that blanket got so dirty. I really can't." Natalie grabs her side, mentions having gas, and then releases it, copious and highly audible, a real conversation stopper, too drawn out and repugnant to be amusing. I turn from her and am delighted to spot a bright blue portable toilet at a construction site only three or four houses away, half of it actually situated on the sidewalk. I point to it gleefully—what a stroke of luck.

"There's usually a fence," Natalie says evenly. "There's always a fence and a padlock." I walk closer to investigate and see that she is right—both the fence and the toilet are in fact double locked. "You have to be careful where you go, anyway," Natalie says. "You don't know what you're liable to pick up in these places. I drank that water till it was gone. Sometimes it makes your stomach stick way out."

She digs beneath the cart for her Sparklett's jug, which I bring home and wash in hot, soapy water before I refill it and take it back, along with a roll of toilet paper and some bread with cheese. Natalie takes a long swig of water and stands by her cart for quite a while chatting in a conversational tone about things that make no sense to me. The tone is sensible, and the individual words and phrases seem coherent on the surface, but the overall message is incomprehensible.

"My father always said don't tell anybody but Ann, and if they come all dressed in black, don't give them anything at all. He was a star of wonder, I guess. Most of them were Daughters of the American Revolution, anyway. But she could ride that horse like nobody's business. You know that yourself."

"What did you say your daughter's name was?" I ask, not that I've forgotten.

"Kathy Marie," she says proudly.

"And your sister's name is Becky?"

"I have a daughter Kathy Marie and a sister Becky and a sister Emily." She grins her toothless grin but refuses to elaborate when I try to find out more. She grabs her side again, grimacing.

"I'm afraid you're sick," I tell her. "Maybe you'll let me get you to a doctor."

"No," Natalie says firmly, straightening herself up. "It's just the tree. I'm tall as a tree, you know."

"You are?"

"Well, I mean I used to be," Natalie says. "Over there on Vermont. And I used to wear armor. Oh, yes. I used to wear that armor. Didn't you ever wear armor?"

"No," I say. "I don't think I did. Maybe I did. I guess I did."

"Well, they all want to see what's inside it, you know." She unzips her jacket partway and points to an inside pocket. "That's where I have to keep the money," she whispers, then rezips, lifts her skirt, and rubs her gloved hands against her knees. "When there's no more cash coming in," she says, "it's time to move along."

| | |

At twilight I look out my window and see the old Goodyear blimp, all lit up in red and green, hovering directly over Natalie. There is an eerie cheerfulness in this, as if Christmas were about to arrive by spaceship. Tonight is the Hollywood parade, and the prayerbook reminds me it's the First Sunday in Advent: "Almighty God, give us grace that we may cast away the works of darkness, and put upon us the armour of light, now in the time of this mortal life, in which thy son Jesus Christ came to visit us in great humility...."

"He was a star of wonder, I guess," Natalie said.

Everybody wants to know what's underneath the armor.

| | NOVEMBER 30

I have worried that the move away from the corner will cut Natalie's prospects for food and caretakers, but I see that two different women have brought offerings to the new location. When I take soup around 5:30, a woman is there with a foil-

covered dish. "Eat it while it's hot, now," she coaxes in a soothing southern accent.

I am always urging Natalie to eat things while they are warm,
too, but this matters much less to her than to me. When I ask if
she wants me to take the soup back home and bring it another
time, she directs me to set it down and assures me she will eat
it cold.

Already the temperature has dropped to the lower fifties,
headed for the mid-forties tonight. I see that Natalie has finally
pulled an extra blanket off her cart to cover with, plus the usual
blanket, plus the plastic sheet spread over herself and all the
bags.

"Are you warm enough?" I ask.

"Oh, yes, it's pretty chilly," she says. She is sitting on one leg
at an angle that looks uncomfortable. "That officer asked me
about this blanket, see. He wanted to know if I stole it, but I told
him it was given to me. It was. It was given to me. I told them
that, too. I mean, I threw a tizzy down there over that."

"How do you like it up here?" I ask. "Is it better than on the
corner?"

"I was soooo tired today," Natalie says. "I slept all day, really.
I was just soooo tired."

"From all that moving," I say. "That was a lot of work."

"Yes, and you have to watch here," she says. "It's not like down
there where you could see people coming." She motions to the
dense, waist-high hedge that her encampment is built against.
While it protects her in a way, it also holds a certain spookiness
after dark.

"That's what I told my son, see."

"You have a son?" I say.

"A cop," she says.

"You have a son who's a cop?"

"Some days he is," Natalie says.

"What's his name?" I ask.

"I've been thirsty," she says. "I don't know why I get so thirsty." Her nose is running, and I offer her a Kleenex, which she takes and uses immediately. Then she reaches behind her for the water I brought yesterday. Nearly half the gallon is gone. "I still have this much left," she says. "So I don't need water. I try not to drink too much. Water is two parts hydrogen and one part oxygen, but then you can't tell what else they're going to put in it. Sometimes lye, sometimes strychnine."

This sharp turn into paranoia makes me realize how grounded she has seemed during this visit, in touch with basic physical reality and speaking with clarity. Just before I leave, though, she plunges into a garbled story about working in a hospital.

"The woman got all congested, you know, and I had to stick that thing down her throat and get that phlegm out of there. On a man and a woman both. But I said, don't tell anybody about that. Don't tell Ann. Don't ever let them know you were that close to death that I had to do it."

| | DECEMBER 1

Natalie is lying down when I stop by around 6:30 p.m. I tell her she needn't sit up, but she does, and she does not look well, by which I mean she looks worse than usual. Maybe it's just the lighting, the yellowish cast from the outdoor lights on the building she's in front of now. This spot is really too public for comfort, even at night, with the lights and the people in and out. The smell is bad today—that clingy, almost palpable mixture of garbage and urine and feces—the odor I sometimes think I can still smell at home, even after careful scrubbing with fragrant soap.

"Have you eaten today?" I ask her.

"He was going to bring me something," Natalie says, "but I guess he got busy and forgot. I'm not that hungry, really. I'm a little hungry, but I don't know what for. Something good. Some salad, maybe."

I don't have any salad makings, don't have much of anything, really, to offer, except boiled eggs.

"And I need water," Natalie adds, reaching back and handing me the container, which has only an inch or so left in it. "I'm so thirsty. I don't know why. I don't know why I'm so terribly thirsty."

"I'll bring water and eggs," I say.

"No, never mind." She reclaims the jug. "Tomorrow will be fine."

"I may not be able to do it tomorrow," I tell her. "But I can do it now." I try to get the container back, but Natalie is holding it firmly against the sidewalk.

"I don't want to drink too much," she says.

"You need to drink. It's good for you. If I'm bringing eggs, I can just as easily bring water." I am losing patience with this perpetual battle between her need for water and her need not to urinate. "Do me a favor and give me the jug."

"No," Natalie says sweetly, "that's all right. I don't require anything more."

| | |

Today's visit was remarkable for its absence of delusional content, though I suppose if I'd stayed on to chat she would soon have been off into something. The move, while it exhausted her and may have weakened her or made her ill, also may have grounded her to reality for a while by requiring her to focus on tangible matters. There is a way in which she is even more heartrending when she is not being delusional—as if somehow the extreme craziness acts as a buffer or distraction from the brutal fact of what she is: a sick and destitute, toothless old woman without shelter, decent diet, means to cleanliness, or hope for change.

| | DECEMBER 2

I deliver coffee on my way to work. Natalie is lying down completely covered—even her head is under the plastic. She sits up groggily to balance the cup. "I woke up earlier," she says. "I combed my hair and looked around and went back to sleep, I can't tell you why."

| | |

In the evening I take orange juice. Natalie's face is grimier than usual, and she has a disoriented look about her, though she is still not muttering or obsessing over paranoid fantasies. Her water jug is full, I see, and when she slips the box of OJ underneath her blanket, I spot a fresh Kentucky Fried Chicken carton stashed away there. I'm relieved she's being fed, but the new campsite is still poorly situated.

"Wouldn't you be more comfortable if we moved you just up the street a bit?" I ask. "So you're not right on this pathway to the building?"

"I was told I could stay here till Friday," Natalie says, her voice rising in defense. "Then I guess they'll come along and turn this cart over and drag everything right back down to the corner where I was in the first place."

"I didn't mean you have to move," I say. "I just mean you might like another spot better. I just thought you might like to have more privacy."

Natalie scrutinizes my face as if I am speaking an unfamiliar language. "That fellow who just went by here with all this and all that," she says. "I don't know if he was high or what. I don't like to be told I'm no good."

As delicately as possible I inquire whether she has any garbage, and without protest she hands over a tightly stuffed, tiny brown sack.

"I ought to have a rearview mirror put on this cart," she says.

| | DECEMBER 3

I had planned a day off from Natalie today, but when I eat less than half of some Stauffer Noodles Romanoff for supper, I can't bring myself to throw it away. I take it, still warm, around seven o'clock. There is fog and mist tonight, blurring a full moon.

Natalie is lying flat when I arrive, and she accepts the dish without enthusiasm, setting it aside without sitting up. It is four days since the move, but still whenever I ask how she is, the answer is always "soooo tired." Tonight she speaks as if exhausted, mumbling and whispering as much to herself as me, conveying the impression that she is on her sickbed and slightly delirious.

"Have you been up at all today?" I ask.

"I tried to take a walk," she says. "But it's better not to, really, you know. I have to be quiet. I try not to make too much noise out here with all these people in and out. Why don't you move up here? Why don't you move down there? I'm telling you, they want what I have. They want to be into everything and get what I have."

"But don't people bring you things?" I ask.

"No," Natalie whispers defiantly. "And I'm not to tell anybody but Ann." She continues mumbling, less and less audibly, until I can't even hear her without leaning close. I can't stand leaning close, though, because of the stench from her and her bags. Fumes—primarily garbage tonight—seem to rise off everything and coagulate in the heavy, damp air, a static, almost tactile phenomenon that brings to mind the wavy lines cartoonists use to indicate bad odors.

"If you want to move over the weekend, I can help you," I say, backing myself to the end of the hedge. "Only if you want to, I mean. I can help you carry your things."

Natalie skillfully ignores me while speaking directly to me. "You remember that big explosion at the Strand, don't you, Ann? When we all had to run up under that porch?"

"No," I say. "I don't remember that."

"Yes you do," Natalie insists. "You remember it like yesterday. And that old what's-her-name, that so-and-so with the red belt. Junie Moon, or whatever her name was. I know you remember that."

"Not really," I say.

"You don't? You don't remember it? This is what I can't believe. It wasn't Junie Moon but a name similar to that. You'll think of it in a minute."

Some days I lack the stomach for dealing with Natalie on the physical level. At times I get a violent urge to grab all her bags and destroy them and force her somehow to shower and put on clean clothes and start over, even if she can't stay in a shelter. It may be this kind of feeling that Natalie picks up from people all the time, which makes her think they want what she has, or at least that they don't want her to have it.

Today at work my friend Kay found Natalie a nice jumper/ sundress that has a pretty, below-the-knee skirt. With a blouse it would be ideal for summer, but it isn't warm enough for now. I don't think Natalie will ever strip, anyway, to put on something new. Draped across my bed, the dress with its bright blue flowers begins to feel oppressive. December itself is threatening to settle into bleakness.

| | DECEMBER 4

My sense of hopelessness about Natalie deepens during the night. At work I begin a serious search for a mental health or social service agency that can come to where a person is (possibly with portable showers and clothing and food). I do find at last a skid row group with a mobile unit, though I'm unsure exactly what its services are. I speak with a worker who asks for a precise location and physical description of Natalie. I emphasize that she is extremely paranoid and unlikely to accept any help that requires her to leave her belongings.

"The sanitation problem is primary right now," I tell him. "And I think she needs medical attention as well as psychiatric. If this woman doesn't qualify as 'gravely disabled,' I'd hate to meet the person who does."

I feel a great relief that someone competent and professional is going to see Natalie, possibly even today, though more likely not until after the weekend.

There is light but relentless rain all day.

| | |

When I get home around 4:30, I see that Natalie has moved camp ten or twelve feet further north and is simply standing idle at her cart, unprotected from the rain. By the time I get there with a couple of soft yellow apples, she is lying down under her plastic, audibly weeping. I have never seen her cry before and can't think of what to say, but Natalie doesn't want my sympathy, anyway, so she declares, or my apples, either. For a second I think she's going to throw them back at me, but instead she sits up on one elbow, holding both apples in one hand, and yells at me for several minutes, crying and swearing and stringing together obscenities.

"Get the fuck away from here," she shouts, but the words are hollow, and I decide to stick with her until she calms down, not an easy thing to do. The neighbors are peeping out their doors to see what's going on—it probably sounds as if I'm torturing her instead of the other way around. Someone came today, but I can't tell whether it was the police or the service van.

"MOVE UP HERE, MOVE DOWN THERE. THE FUCKERS JUST WON'T LEAVE YOU ALONE. AND ASKING ME IF I DON'T WANT TO WASH IN THE RAIN. HOW STUPID CAN YOU GET? THEY SAID EVERY TIME I HAD A BOWEL MOVEMENT TO MOVE FARTHER UP THE STREET. BUT I DON'T KNOW WHERE TO GO. CAN'T THEY SEE I'VE MOVED? CAN'T YOU SEE I *HAVE* MOVED? CAN'T YOU SEE I'M WET?"

I offer a Kleenex, which Natalie takes without comment, wiping away tears and blowing her nose before she resumes shouting.

"DON'T TELL ANYBODY ANYTHING. DON'T TELL THEM, DON'T TELL THEM, DON'T TELL THEM. THEY COME HERE WITH THIS GERMAN, SAYING SHE'S YOUR FRIEND AND THIS AND THAT. SHE'S NOT MY FRIEND! ARE YOU CRAZY OR WHAT?"

This remark sets off my own paranoia—could the social worker have mentioned my name and told Natalie that I called him? I'm upset that this might be the case and even more upset that his visit seems only to have made things worse. As it starts to rain harder, Natalie winds down into quiet weeping.

"People don't understand how I have to live," she says. "The people who have places to stay don't understand how I have to live. You have a place to stay, Ann. They don't understand that. I *have* moved. The blanket was given to me, but it's wet now, anyway, so what do they care about it?"

I speak calmly, as if her yelling hasn't occurred. "A lot of people think you're a good person, Natalie, and a lot of people love you."

"I know they do," she says, and I believe she means it.

"That's why they want you to go someplace inside where you can be warm and dry and have food and nice, clean clothes. They care about you, so they want you taken care of. They want you to have a place to stay."

"You can eat these," Natalie says, offering the apples. "Don't you want these for yourself?"

I assure her that I don't, that she can have them if she wants them or throw them away if she doesn't want them.

"Well, they're nice ones," she says. "I ate that persimmon and that V-8 juice, but I don't know. He doesn't want me to eat too much. I didn't put on those men's pants. I have to be careful about that."

The rain is blowing harder, soaking through my sweatpants as I bend to listen.

"I have to go, Natalie," I say. "My rear end is getting drenched out here."

"You need an umbrella," she observes, lifting her plastic cover toward me. "I wish I could give you one of these, really."

"That's all right," I say. "You need that. I have a place to stay, remember? I hate to leave you out here like this."

"I have the apples," she says. "And I had that cup of soup before."

| | |

A thunderstorm is brewing tonight with a hard-blowing downpour. Since moving from the corner Natalie has been on an incline, and now water is running down the sidewalk and soaking everything underneath her, even though the plastic keeps the rain directly off. She is still in front of the same apartment building, just a bit further from the entrance, closer to the impenetrable toilet at the construction site.

"I was told I could stay here till Friday," she said after her initial move, and I wonder now whether the cops came back to shoo her on today. Somehow I don't think the social workers would have insisted she move, though Natalie might well have taken that as the message, no matter what they said. Seeing her cry makes me realize how brave and strong she is most of the time, and how remarkably free of self pity. In addition to the danger and discomfort of getting cold and wet, there is the humiliation, something tied into our folksy notion of "not having sense enough to come in out of the rain," along with the humiliation of, as my father would put it, "not having a pot to piss in or a window to throw it out of."

| | December 5

I sleep with my window open and watch and listen to the rain on and off all night, cozy under heavy covers. Except for knowing Natalie isn't dry, I take great pleasure in the cool, damp air and the sound of water gentle (at last) upon the palms.

I carry coffee as I head up the hill to jog. Natalie is lying under a soaking blanket beneath a sheet of plastic. Her furry coat lining, which she has always kept between herself and the concrete, is now on top of the cart, also saturated. She is glad for the coffee and is less concerned about all the wetness or catching a chill than about having soiled her skirt.

"You have to crouch like an animal," she says, reaching back to show me a styrofoam cup, not quite covered with foil. "It looks like chocolate pudding. Don't eat it."

I promise to come back with a sack for it later. This is strong stuff before breakfast, but I don't think concepts like "before breakfast" or "after lunch" hold much meaning for Natalie at this point. Everything seems to have slipped from terrible to worse overnight.

"These laundromats all want a balanced load," she says. "And they won't allow for the bending of coins. You can't wash wool or I'd have washed this skirt."

| | |

Around 11 a.m. I take clean underpants and heavy knee socks and bags for the waste. Natalie is huddled under her plastic and tries to uncover a bit when I arrive but decides it's too cold to move around. I slip the socks and pants inside her tent and she manages, with some delicacy, to hand me the cup.

"Abraham Street," she mutters, and the mention of it seems to launch her into a stream of tales, the usual intense combination of delusion and memory and defensive fantasy. "He loved the men, all right, and he was jealous if I even looked at one. I'll never go to a doctor like that one. Honey, they stick this thing down your throat and they put something in it, lye or something. It messes up your innards like you would not believe. And with him going up behind all the time and cutting this and that, here and there, you know. Do you know what a scratch pad is? You know what I'm talking about, don't you?"

"I can't hear everything you say," I tell her. "Do you mean stretch pants?"

"SCRATCH PAD, SCRATCH PAD," she enunciates loudly. She has mentioned scratch pads before as part of another indecipherable narrative. "There are different sizes," she says. "Some are four by seven, some of them are three by five. And that's what I went in there to get. I'm talking about Abraham Street now. But that man and woman at the Hotel St. Mary's that time. She wanted him in her, see. You know, his penis. And I went on up to the room and done what he said. You know. But then he was up her ass and everything else."

I take my leave abruptly, knowing that these ramblings never conclude on their own. I leave her with the underpants and socks in hand, lying flat on bare, wet concrete, underneath the plastic with her bags of garbage. The day is gray and still and unlikely to dry out much.

| | |

Mid-afternoon I drive to a thrift shop on Normandie and search through stacks and racks of stale and undesirable clothing, finding at last a skirt that may do for Natalie—right length, right style, right size, and very dark brown in color. Perfect except that it's cotton when it should be wool for warmth.

"Would you be willing to make a donation of this?" I ask the man at the register. "It's for a street woman not too far away from here. She's sick and her clothes got wet."

"We set our prices low," the man says. His head is so large that it looks to me as if his Dodger-blue cap may be cutting off circulation. His face appears to contain massive bones that don't allow for much animation of flesh. "It's only two-twenty-five," he says. "I can hold it here at the desk for you." He's assessed my new ten-dollar Pic-n-Save sweater and decided I have money.

"It's not for me," I say. "It's for a bag lady on my street. I just thought you might be able to help out."

"Why doesn't she come on over herself?" the man says. "We've been known to make an exception. You can't make the exception every time."

"Never mind," I say, unzipping my purse.

"Which car out there is yours?" he asks, peering through the dirty plate glass. "Did I see you drive that yellow Bug in here? I know a guy who can straighten out that rear fender for you. In about five minutes, too. No ifs, ands, or buts."

"No thanks," I say, offering exact change.

"Keep it," the man says. "We've been known to make an exception. Like I say, you just can't make the exception every time."

"Right," I agree. "Then it wouldn't be an exception at all."

"Exactly," he says. "That's exactly right. Now you're picking up on what I mean. It wouldn't be an exception if you did it all the time. This rain is something else, you think?" He wants to carry the skirt to the car for me, an offer I politely decline.

As I approach Natalie, a little blonde girl clutching a doll is standing right alongside her, staring at her through the plastic sheet. In a moment the mother appears, whisking the child away just as a tall Caucasian man hurries past, grinning broadly, as if the sight of Natalie somehow amuses him. I show her the skirt to distract her from this, but my enthusiasm seems to hit her wrong and sets her off full volume.

"I CAN'T CHANGE CLOTHES OUT HERE IN DAYLIGHT WITH A KID AND MEN AND WOMEN WALKING BY."

"You can do it later," I say quietly. "Just take a look at it. I think it might work out."

"I HAD THAT DAMN THING WHEN I WAS JUST A KID," she shouts, eyeing the skirt with contempt. "I DON'T WANT TO WEAR THESE OLD THINGS PEOPLE HAVE HAD AGAINST THEIR BODIES. SOME OLD TRASH SOMEBODY WANTS TO THROW AWAY."

"It's clean," I say. "Dammit, Natalie."

"SOMETHING THEY STOLE OFF YOUR CART IN THE FIRST PLACE AND THEN BRING IT BACK TO YOU LIKE IT WAS SOMETHING DIFFERENT. THEY RAM IT RIGHT UP YOUR ASSHOLE, TOO."

"So you don't want me to leave the skirt," I say, as furious as she is.

"GO AHEAD AND LEAVE IT," Natalie shouts, dismissing me with a swipe of her palm.

"I don't want to leave it if you're not going to wear it," I say.

"TURN THE CART OVER AND TAKE IT ALL," she yells. "GO AHEAD. HE'LL BE UP YOUR ASS, TOO."

"I paid for it, dammit," I lie. I feel as if I did pay for it.

"WELL, I PAID FOR MINE, TOO," she says nastily. "AND THEY TOOK IT AND WIPED UP THE STREET WITH IT."

"Wonderful," I say, just as nasty back. "I give up, Natalie. You win. Keep on wearing the one with shit. It's great. Don't ever take it off. Wear it till the goddamn thing rots." I fold up the skirt and charge home with it, leaving her soaking and stinking and muttering accusations.

| | December 6

I am spending this gray and chilly day in my study, on the inner side of the apartment, close to the heat, away from all north windows, protected by two walls from the wounding sight of Natalie. She has worn me out, or rather I've worn myself out, anger and frustration superimposed now over sadness. At the simplest, most embarrassing level, I'm outraged that I can't make her do what I want her to do "for her own good." Ironically, Natalie has at her mercy all of us who want to help her. How dare she stubbornly persist in causing us to suffer? Certainly one major aim of lunatic asylums has always been to isolate disturbed people, because they disturb those of us who appear or pretend or aspire to be ruled by reason. I so much want Natalie out of my sight today that I'm questioning my own motives for wanting her hospitalized. I tell myself I'd want someone to do the same for me, but even the Golden Rule betrays an egocentric slant: why not do unto others as they would have you do, rather than "as you would have them do unto you"?

Roy Porter has suggested that the history of madness is the history of power, that madness, in its bold imagining of power, is both impotence and omnipotence. Why such a blatant feeling yesterday that Natalie had "won," that I had been "defeated"? On the surface she "won" the dubious privilege of continuing to wear her own horrid skirt instead of changing into a clean one. Actually, she won a chance to express her anger at her situation by not improving it, thereby asserting her right to self-determination.

When I pulled into the gas station this morning, a man in dirty and disheveled clothing had situated himself carefully on the concrete island of pumps, leaning slightly into one, arms folded, waiting for me.

"Good morning, Miss," he says as I get out of the car.

"Good morning," I say. I know he will ask for something when I return from the cashier, and I decide to say no, decide I have nothing to give today. In my absence he moves from the center pump to the one I plan to use, so as I lift the nozzle to switch it on he is nearly breathing in my face.

"I could pump that for you, Miss," he says, and he seems for the moment both sane and sober.

"No thanks," I say, though I am struggling with the gas cap because I didn't unlock it before I picked up the hose.

"I can get it for you," he says again.

"I've got it, thanks," I tell him. His undertone is only slightly menacing, layered over with polite friendliness. He is making himself just intimidating enough that it would be easier to give in than to refuse him.

"I'm trying to earn eighty-five cents to get a bus downtown," he says. "That's all I need more is eighty-five cents, if you could help me out."

"Not today," I say, friendly and polite myself to cover my uneasiness. "I can't do it today."

"I could pump that for you for eighty-five cents."

I decline again, politely, thinking, "Goddammit, why do you think I'm at the self-serve in the first place, if not to save money?"

"Somebody dropped me off over here," he says, barely not whining. "Now I got no way to get back downtown. I can't get me no check or no shelter or nothing if I don't get back downtown."

"I said I can't do it today." I stonewall him, annoyed now and determined.

"Well, hell, some other day I prob'ly won't need it. This is the day I need it."

"Then ask somebody else," I say.

"Shit, girl. Nobody 'round here even speaks English. It's Chinese or it's Korean or it's Spanish or some other shit. I finally find somebody who speaks English and she won't even help me out." (This is a cleverly twisted tug on Caucasian guilt—black and white have to stick together now as true-born Americans in the face of L.A.'s burgeoning immigrant population.)

"Maybe you should start walking," I tell him, clutching bills and change in my hand as I hang up the hose. "It's not that far downtown, really."

"Sheee-*it*!" he says. "I don't believe it. You don't look like you'd be that way. A lousy eighty-five cents. Nobody else even speaks English over here. What the hell am I supposed to do?"

"I don't know," I say, getting into the car. "I don't know what you're supposed to do."

I can feel him watching me drive off. I "won" this one. He was absolutely certain he could make me give him a dollar bill. But winning this game makes me feel as drained and lousy as losing.

| | DECEMBER 7

The chilliness continues, and there has been more rain. Even with my windows closed last night, I couldn't stay warm enough to sleep, finally resorting to turning the heat on low, then waking in a sweat two hours later, turning it off, and starting the cycle over again. Natalie has moved her camp another ten or fifteen feet north, farther up the hill, in front of the small house that sits adjacent to the vacant lot. Mostly she lies flat beneath her plastic, though early this morning she sat up to comb her hair, the one bit of grooming she seems able to sustain. I am irked at myself for dawdling with coffee—by the time I called the agency downtown, the mobile unit had already gone into the field for the day, so I could get no word on whether they've seen Natalie yet or if they intend to see her.

Today I won't leave the house. Today I need a hideaway, having lost touch with even the slight capacity I have for what the Buddhists call "joyous participation in the sorrows of the world." Lately I am starved for tenderness, which always turns me into something of a porcupine. Sometimes loneliness is the price that solitude exacts, even the most carefully chosen solitude. May Sarton suggests that being oneself involves so much ruthlessness toward others that very few people can afford it. I think a certain ruthlessness toward the self is required, as well, which is why most of us are so willing to settle for less.

Weeks ago I splurged on a new *American Heritage Dictionary*, an updated college edition of my old favorite from 1969. I must have been saving it for this rainy day—cutting away the cellophane feels like opening a present. "The single source for people who need to be right," the cover proclaims (I guess we know who we are). The back cover boasts of "200,000 graceful, full-sentence definitions" with "meanings you most often want listed first," 3,000 photographs and illustrations, and 800 usage notes, plus, among several other items, synonym paragraphs discriminating subtle differences and *thousands* of new words. This is all a bit overwhelming, in concert with the stiffness of the binding and the crisp-cut, gold-lettered thumb index. The thing is "user friendly," though, and I'm delighted immediately with the revelation that a *hermit* is not merely "a person who has withdrawn from society and lives a solitary existence," but also "a spiced cookie made with molasses, raisins, and nuts." A *hermitage* is described as "the habitation of a hermit or group of hermits" or "a place where one can live in seclusion" or "the condition or way of life of a hermit." One appreciates this graceful thoroughness only upon discovering that the *Oxford American* defines *hermitage* as merely a "hermit's dwelling place." *American Heritage* describes *recluse* (a word I've cared for ever since learning in my Mississippi high school that Emily Dickinson was a "New England recluse") as "a person who withdraws from the world to live in solitude and seclusion." This sounds so much more tolerable and healthy and appealing than the harsh assessment in the *Oxford* as "a person who lives alone and avoids mixing with people."

I am disappointed that among the thousands of new scientific or technical entries I do not find *decompensation*, psychological jargon that refers generally to the severe worsening of psychotic symptoms. This is what seems to be happening to Natalie on the street now as she becomes less and less able to order her thoughts and behavior or to interact or communicate in a conventionally meaningful or sensible way. I've never understood specifically how *de*compensation applies to this condition, but I do find an entry in my paperback *Random House* that is illuminating if not precise: *decompensation* is "the inability of a diseased heart to compensate for its defect," which perhaps holds true for a diseased mind as well.

I've got the makings for split-pea soup if I skip the sausage, which I will do rather than face a supermarket (superagora-phobia). I can make a skillet of cornbread, too. The trick, I've finally learned, is in getting the skillet and oil hot enough first, so the batter crispens as you pour it in. Miraculously, I am able to think about these things. My mind can imagine them and plan them out, and my body can understand and then accomplish what is required, can accomplish it perfectly, really, viewed in a certain light.

Maybe by tomorrow I can carry food up the hill again.

| | DECEMBER 8

Calling the downtown agency right at 8 a.m. I am able to catch Victor, the outreach worker I spoke with last week. He and another man, a therapist, saw Natalie yesterday afternoon. I am surprised to learn that she talked with them for nearly half an hour, responding appropriately to their questions, despite a lot of delusional material. It must have been the police, then, who upset her so on Friday. I don't fully realize the burden Natalie has been for me until I let it sink in that she now has a connection with two competent and caring professional people—my relief is so sudden that it leaves me light-headed. According to formal assessment, Natalie does qualify as "gravely disabled," and they are hoping to get her hospitalized, possibly even by the end of this week, a piece of joyful news I find difficult to believe at first—I have to ask the gentle-voiced Victor to repeat himself. Of course, we both acknowledge that in all likelihood she will be discharged back to the street in two or three weeks, but still, if this plan works, she will be warm and dry and clean and fed and cared for medically, at least through the Christmas holidays.

| | |

I decide I will take Natalie some food around noon and then not see her much the rest of the week in the hope that my withdrawal of support might help her move toward accepting hospitalization. On the way up with soup and cornbread I run into May, out for one of her brisk and purposeful, behatted walks. She is glad to hear my news, especially since Natalie's most recent campsite is directly across the street from her own apartment building. She reports that Natalie has been ranting and raving much of the time since this move, shouting unrepeatable obscenities and generally making a nuisance of herself.

"She needs to go for her own safety," May says. "It's not for food. You can look at her and see she doesn't want for food. But there have been these recent attacks, you know, on bag ladies in particular. One murder that I know of. And then one beating where he slashed her ankles. I'm afraid this one's going to sit over there and say the wrong thing to the wrong one some of these times. She does have quite the mouth, you know. Oh yes, she does, indeed."

As I approach Natalie is perched on her styrofoam ice chest, her skirt gathered into a wad in her lap, revealing pale, thin legs that are immodestly (and uncharacteristically) open. She is, as May said, ranting and raving, and the look in her eye is wild. She does not greet me or give any sign of recognition, and I have to interrupt her yelling to offer the food.

"I don't know if I should take it or not," she says. "I'm so sick inside." She appears to resent this intrusion that requires a rational decision, but in a moment she motions for me to set the cup and plate down on the (still wet) blanket bunched at her feet. As soon as I accomplish this, the shouting resumes, her usual brand of stuff only now at top volume—obscene scenarios that involve anal rape and forced fellatio, murder and mayhem and mutilation. In time all this winds down into one repetitive image which she seems unable to get past.

"SUCKING OFF A DOG IN THE PARLOR," she screams. "SUCKING A DOG'S PENIS IN THE PARLOR. SUCKING A DOG IN THE PARLOR AND DON'T-TELL-DON'T-TELL-DON'T-TELL. CAN'T YOU UNDERSTAND WHAT I MEAN? SUCKING OFF A DOG IN THE PARLOR? DO YOU UNDERSTAND THAT?"

"Yeah, yeah, yeah," I say in a feeble attempt to quiet her.

"Yeah, yeah, yeah," she mocks. "You don't understand a goddamn thing, do you? I'M TALKING ABOUT SUCKING A DOG OFF IN THE PARLOR. A DOG'S PENIS IN THE PARLOR. SUCKING A DOG. Don't you even see what I mean?"

Oddly it's "in the parlor" that makes this unbearable to hear—degradation in the midst of refinement, evoking either baroque pornographic fantasy or an actual home of horrors. "In the parlor" is not to be lightly dismissed.

I step back a bit from the assault of words as a shift in breeze stirs up the fierce odor from Natalie's clothing and from a fly-covered paper bag beside her ice chest. Suddenly she is grumbling something about filthy Japs at the Korean gardener who has arrived to tidy up the yard she's camped in front of.

"Why don't you move here, why don't you move there? This Jap comes out with a sprinkler wanting me to move. Where am

I supposed to go? What does he want me to do about it? I can't help it. If it's over this blanket, this blanket belongs to me. I told him that already. I can't help it if he doesn't believe me." The man sweeps quickly, then disappears inside a shed. Natalie begins her litany of places she has stayed and the horrific things she suffered there—arsenic and lye and strychnine down the throat, sexual abuse, assault, the usual variety of cataclysmic explosions.

"Timbuktu over here on St. Francis Place. That was old Virginia. You know Virginia? Hell, you don't know anything. She was the main one behind it, the one that lit up the wicker herself."

"I'm hoping maybe you'll be able to go to a hospital sometime." I say this very quietly, and I believe from the spark in her eye that Natalie registers it before she resumes her rant.

"I don't mean a hospital," she says defiantly. "I'm not talking about a hospital. I mean over there with that Virginia the virgin. Rammed it right down my throat...." She trails off at last, sighing and wiping away with her sleeve the copious white spittle that has accumulated at the corners of her mouth. "There was a fellow yesterday," she begins softly. "There were a couple of fellows here yesterday...."

I wait, but she doesn't finish, and I don't want to set her off again by probing. She watches blankly as I leave, and I feel as if there has been no real contact. From the foot of the hill she appears to be floating on styrofoam amid her vast black and white sea of bags.

| | DECEMBER 9

After work I walk up to see if Natalie is still there. I find her lying down, nearly buried under plastic and debris, but her eyes are open, and she has regained a measure of sanity. She recognizes me, even seems glad to see me.

"How are you today?" I ask. "Do you need anything?"

Natalie laughs and answers softly. "I guess I always need something, don't I? I'm sorry I was so irritable the other day. But when that man is after you and after you, sometimes you just can't take it anymore."

"I know you get really angry out here," I say. "I know you can't help it sometimes."

"You got new glasses," Natalie says. "I didn't know you went to the optometrist."

"They're not new," I tell her. "I just don't usually have them on when I come up here to visit."

"Well, I didn't know you had them. Did you see the sky this morning?"

I did, as a matter of fact, see the sky at sunrise, which was extraordinarily pink and beautiful. It was the light itself that woke me up—as perhaps it did Natalie.

"All that pink," she says, gesturing broadly toward the east. "And those clouds all along there everywhere."

"It was gorgeous, wasn't it?" I say.

"Boy, it sure was." Her eyes are shining, though everything else about her is dulled with grime. I am thrilled that we are having this "normal" conversation—that Natalie noticed something lovely, was moved, remembered it, can talk about it with me. "Did you get some sleep last night?" she asks.

How does she know I haven't been sleeping well? Circles under the eyes? Do I look as depleted as I feel?

"I know this is the 10th," she says. "Let's see. I know this is the 10th."

"Actually, it's the 9th," I say.

"Oh, yes," Natalie says. "December the 9th. I know sometimes after December the 10th a store will be open and these people that work in the stores, you know, they'll have to work late and they get awfully tired."

"Yes," I say. "The stores stay open later at Christmastime. They want to take in all the money they can." This conversation appears to make sense, but I'm not sure what we're discussing.

"It's hard sometimes," Natalie says, "when you can't just do what you like. Of course, none of us can ever really just do as we please."

"That's true," I say. "We sure can't."

"But I know that Neiman Marcus used to stay open a lot later," she says. "It's hard when you aren't able to do what you want to do."

"You have a lot of extra burdens out here," I say.

"Yes, I do," Natalie says firmly. "I certainly do. But I thank my Heavenly Father." She crosses herself several times. "I thank my Heavenly Father, and I thank the Blessed Mother. I do, I thank the Blessed Mother. Some say don't, you know. My mother was always don't you do that, you get away from there. But Ann-Margret. Excuse me, but I mean Ann-Margret, wearing that little suit, you know, like a tuxedo, and a top hat? Moving it this way and that way? You know?"

I say that I do know, and we have quite an extended chuckle over Ann-Margret, swinging our imaginary canes back and forth, though Natalie is still lying flat on her back.

"I'm so glad you're feeling calmer today," I tell her. "I'm hoping maybe you'll be in someplace warm for Christmas."

"Well, I'm not looking that far ahead myself," Natalie says, dismissing the idea.

"I mean I hope if you ever get a chance to go to a hospital that you'll take the opportunity and go," I say.

"They all want to know what we two have in common," she whispers. "They're all curious about why we're friends, but I think it's mostly jealousy, don't you?"

"Could be," I say. Someone has given her two thick and sturdy sofa cushions, but they are lying on top of the bags at her feet instead of underneath her. "Why don't we make you a good bed out of these?" I suggest. "Let me help you arrange them before I go."

"You're much too tired for that," Natalie says. "You've already done too much."

"I'm not that tired," I say. "Maybe you're the one too tired to move."

She turns onto her side, away from me, as if she's about to go to sleep. "He doesn't allow those pillows where my body is, honey. Some things are very strict. It wouldn't be worth the trouble it would cause, believe me. You have no idea what can happen after dark."

I stand for a moment, looking at her from behind. I may not see her again, hope not to see her again, in fact, and I feel as if there should be some parting words, but I can't feel what they are. I start down the hill, then turn back.

"God bless you, Natalie," I say. She doesn't respond or acknowledge this, and I don't have the heart to repeat it.

I I DECEMBER 10

I am disappointed to see that Natalie is still there when I get home from work. Surely tomorrow they'll pick her up. Or maybe they came today and she refused to go along—a distinct possibility, if not probability. I think I won't visit, but then I do, carrying water and orange juice and a cup of soup. She is grateful and very polite today—when a drop of soup splashes onto her (unspeakably filthy) glove, she draws in a sharp breath and whispers "Excuse me" in dramatic, formal-dinner tones.

"How's it going?" I ask. "Did you have any visitors today?"

"Oh, all he does is keep bugging me about you," she says, sounding eager to confide some delicious gossip. "They all say who is she to you, and what do we have in common? Are you lesbians? You know, this is how they talk. They ask me this and that. He wants to know why we spend time together. Jealous, you see. They don't like it one bit." She looks at me for a response, but I keep neutral, not about to encourage elaboration on this intriguing little scenario. "It's hard to know how to manage everything sometimes," Natalie continues. "You should hear them talk. And when somebody is just beating you and beating you until you hurt inside, hitting you right above your little herpes, you know...." She points precisely and emphatically through her skirt, indicating she must mean her clitoris. "When they hit you that hard right on here, it hurts, let me tell you. But boy, it got cold here last night, too. I'm glad you were inside all night, though, weren't you?"

"Yes," I say. "I have a place to stay. I like to stay inside."

"So-and-so, Esquire," she says. "They put that on these cards they give out. Kind of like an equestrian, or whatever you want to call it. Equestrian, or something like that. That's it, equestrian." She speaks as if she has surprised herself with this word she doesn't own.

"An equestrian is someone who rides a horse," I say, which seems to resonate for her.

"Oh yes, oh yes," she grins. "Those policemen, too. There'll be an equestrian here or there, I suppose."

"Equestrian," I say. We get into a giggle over the word, which sounds funnier each time one of us repeats it. Suddenly Natalie turns serious and motions me closer so she can whisper in my ear.

"They claim the ones in England don't carry a gun, but they'll beat the living whey out of you with those sticks," she says. "Equestrian or not doesn't matter to them. You know what a scratch pad is, don't you, Ann?"

"Yes," I say. "I know what it is."

"I thought you did," Natalie says, relieved. "I knew you did, really. I don't know why I asked you that."

"That's all right," I say. "But I need to go get some supper now and let you eat your soup."

"Thanks an awful lot, honey. I'm sorry I spilled that cup. I wouldn't have done that for the world if I could help it. You have a nice night now."

"If I don't see you tomorrow, Natalie, remember I love you,"
I say.

"Well...OK." She is grinning broadly beneath her blue cap but
looks at my feet instead of my face. "You have a nice day and a
nice night both," she says.

I start off backwards, thinking she might look up and wave or
something, but she is busy rummaging for the plastic spoon I
brought, balancing the styrofoam cup on her knee.

I I DECEMBER 11

I am more than disappointed to find Natalie still ensconced on
the hill as I drive in from work. A heavy mantle of hopelessness
settles over me at the sight of her, and by the time I get inside
the apartment I have to cry. I've reached the point now where
the mere thought of her is painful, the actual vision excruciat-
ing. Victor said *maybe* they could pick her up by today, but I've
been counting on it absolutely. He isn't in when I call the agency,
and the woman I speak to tells me that Natalie was not on the
visit list today.

"But he was hoping to have her hospitalized by now," I say.
There is a pleading in my voice that makes me wish I hadn't
called.

"Oh, I see," the woman says sympathetically. "There haven't
been any open beds all week. There's no way he could have gotten her in this week. Not a chance. Maybe next week. I'll have
him call you back next week for sure."

"I feel so discouraged," I tell her. "I thought the arrangements had already been made."

"Well, I know," she says, kind and resigned. "It's a very discouraging situation we're working with here."

| | DECEMBER 12

A clear and beautiful, windy winter day, early winter, that is, and winter for Los Angeles. The temperature won't rise above the middle sixties, but the air at least is dry. Mid-afternoon I see Natalie moving camp back down the hill to where she was two sites ago, in front of the apartment building. Apparently it is the beginning of construction on the empty lot that has driven her to this—today there are trucks and bulldozers with their accompanying crews and lots of noise. Natalie negotiates many, many trips downhill with her umpteen bags and her cart and her cushions and her covers. She moves slowly, often stopping to rest on her feet, casting hostile glances back at the workmen as she relinquishes territory to them. She has words I can't hear with the Korean gardener she called "Jap" the other day, and then he proceeds to hose down the sidewalk where she was camped, even while some of her belongings remain. The little five- or six-year-old girl who has stared at Natalie before stands staring at her now for a time, half hidden behind the hedge that will again provide a makeshift wall to live against.

Soon the Black woman who gave Natalie money and spoke with me about shelter appears. I can tell by her body language even this far away that she is trying to "reason" with Natalie, while Natalie is being her defiant self. When Mrs. Atkins puts her hands on her hips, Natalie does the same. Mrs. Atkins points her finger emphatically west while Natalie gazes directly east. Eventually, though, Natalie does follow her into the yard of the apartment complex to continue the conversation, which is either a bad or good sign. I hope Mrs. Atkins is savvy enough to keep her distance, in case Natalie tries to lash out, but the women part without incident, and Natalie continues her gradual relocation. She walks slowly, holding her side with one hand, carrying stuff with the other. The sofa cushions come next to last, then all the plastic covering and she's done. I am surprised to see her choose a bag and walk down the apartment complex driveway with it, perhaps to the rear of the building to throw it away. Maybe this is what Mrs. Atkins spoke to her about, getting rid of "trash." Natalie is gone for several minutes and then, sure enough, reappears without the bag, ready to settle down. Witnessing this superficially rational act cheers me up. Natalie is still using the large cushions as boundary markers for her camp rather than as a bed.

I don't dare go up today, might weep if she yelled at me or weep if she were sweet. I am weepy anyway, with cramps and the dark weight of Christmas futility. By sundown there is a chilly, hard-blowing wind and a gathering of clouds. The radio says down to forty tonight with gusts up to forty-five miles an hour. I close all the windows, wrap up, and turn the heat on high.

| | DECEMBER 13

It did get close to forty last night, and wind is still hissing through the palms this morning. A wind-chill factor is not something you figure on in L.A., but so far this year five or six deaths among the homeless population have been linked to cold weather. Now the city sets up emergency shelters during these drastic cold snaps and, responding to public pressure, even opens up City Hall itself, a gesture more symbolic than practical. Natalie is sitting under plastic, huddled against her cart, her extra blankets piled high out of reach as usual.

At work we have a client now who is as chronically and seriously ill as Natalie except that she suffers from the undifferentiated type of schizophrenia, rather than the paranoid type, and so is not paralyzed by delusions of persecution and victimization. This woman is also a "hardcore bag lady" who has managed to disturb and disrupt her chosen westside business-corner neighborhood to the point where the local councilman insisted that she *had* to be admitted *somewhere* in the mental health system. Two social workers finally coaxed her in. Because she has been the subject of media attention, political image is at stake all around. The woman so far has no verifiable name, date of birth, or social security number. She calls herself Joan Doe, though I notice she sometimes signs herself Lady Jane Doe, too. Joan, who appears robust except for a severe, hacking smoker's cough, looks to be in her middle fifties. She assures us that Madonna is her very best friend; that the U.C.L.A. campus is to be avoided because it is permeated with the odor of embalming fluid; that Myrna Loy sends her messages constantly, either by telepathy or television; and that she herself comes "from a different walk of life" and has been sent here on a mission to save the starving people of the world. This is Joan's third brief stay in our program—twice before she has left on her own and made her way back to her westside corner, which is most likely where she'll end up this time, too, confounding everyone's best efforts and intentions to get her not only cared for but also out of sight. Natalie's prognosis may be much the same except she is older and weaker, more frightened and helpless than "Lady Jane," who grandiosely declared one board-and-care facility too "insubstantial" for her because "it looks exactly like a hotel where no people in show business would ever want to stay." Natalie's convinced she'll get lye down her throat in such a place, but the ultimate effect of the disease is the same for both women—life on the streets.

I still don't have the heart for a visit today and am grateful to catch sight of Mrs. Atkins handing Natalie a bowl of something around noon.

| | |

I drive out to visit my friend Robert in Venice, and we spend the entire afternoon walking the boardwalk and bike path, from his place to the Venice pier and back again and then all the way to the Santa Monica palisades. It is a stunningly clear and beautiful day because of the wind, and the beach is uncrowded because of the cold. I am comfortable with three layers of clothing including a turtleneck and cap. By the time we head back for dinner, the sun has disappeared, taking with it the tourists.

Near Rose Avenue a bedraggled and ill-clad woman in her thirties approaches us for money. The people in tents along the beach there have been told to break camp in exchange for hotel vouchers or rides to distant shelters, but some have refused and plan to sit tight until the January 1 deadline, when an ordinance against their remaining will be fully enforced. After several police sweeps and crackdowns in Skid Row Los Angeles, the ranks of visibly homeless people in Venice increased so much that city officials felt obliged to call for tougher laws banning them from public beaches, where they are said to pose a dire menace to tourism, to astronomically inflated property values, and to the restaurant business. Dispersal seems to be the favored solution everywhere, though other proposals and experiments here have included tent cities, urban campgrounds, dog kennel conversions, and the purchase of two thousand trailers. Somebody offered an old barge that would hold four hundred people (if only an acceptable—or accepting—docking place could be found). Then there was the Pope's visit, including a trek around town in his bulletproof Popemobile, which necessitated the "displacement" of "transients" downtown to "accommodations" in a large city warehouse for "security" reasons.

"Watch the special on Channel 11," the beach woman keeps telling us over and over. "When they tore down the tents they took my epilepsy medicine and blankets and everything else. It's a crime the way they did us. There's a special about it on Channel 11. Watch that special and you'll see what I mean." She reeks of booze, and at the first sniff of it Robert and I exchange a look as he digs in his jeans for money—we both know the exact day, month, and year of our last drink.

"I wouldn't ask you except it's for food," she says, reading us accurately. "They steal everything away down here."

I mention the names and nearby locations of several agencies where she can get free meals or groceries and other help.

"I been there," she says abruptly. "I been there a hundred times. Everything is such a hassle. Watch that special tonight on Channel 11, I'm not kidding. It's on. You'll see it, and then you'll see I was right. Channel 11, don't forget. If you forget, you'll miss it." She isn't shivering but should be, in a thin cotton dress with no jacket or sweater, practically barefoot in battered thongs.

"If you're having any psychiatric problems, I know another place where you can stay," I tell her. "You can't drink there, but you can see a doctor and get everything you need."

"I'm not mentally ill," the woman says, creasing Robert's dollar bill carefully into eighths. "What do you think I am, crazy? They got it even worse. I'm homeless, sure, but I'm not crazy. I have a B.A. in psychology myself, but who would hire me dressed like this? Be sure to watch that program. It's a special all about this stuff you're talking about. Really. You'll enjoy it." She thanks us and heads off limping across the sand, then disappears behind the scattered cars left in the public lot.

On TV the other night Robert and I both heard a stand-up comic joke about "a bum on Venice Beach" who asked him for money for a bottle of wine. "Oh, I don't know," the punchline went. "How can I be sure you won't go out and spend it all on food?" We live in a time and place, historically and geographically and spiritually, where this gets a very big laugh. I don't think Channel 11 will be running a special on that. (I discover, in fact, that Channel 11 isn't running any specials at all.)

Reality and realty. In law, *real* means property that is stationary and fixed, like land or buildings. The tents on the beach aren't *real*, obviously, and what I own myself is no more *real* than Natalie's shopping cart. Some time ago a woman repeatedly rammed the van in which she was living into the front of a posh restaurant on the Venice boardwalk, declaring she was tired of the owner calling homeless people "bums." Attacking a building like that must be what constitutes *real* crime.

| | DECEMBER 14

It is 38° at 8 a.m., though finally the winds have ceased. Victor's phone call jars me out of bed, and we have a hurried, somewhat disjointed conversation, me shivering and half asleep, him having been out on the streets of skid row all yesterday and most of the night distributing blankets and trying to entice some of his regular patients into temporary shelters. At this point he sounds as if he's operating on the manic energy that masks exhaustion, and I feel concerned for him.

"Shouldn't you be taking the day off now?" I ask.

"No way today," he says. "Too much going on down here." He hasn't forgotten Natalie but was unable to get back to her last week. "Maybe I can see her today," he says. "Or maybe Wednesday. We have to wait for a designated-unit bed before we can make a move."

I feel heartened by this and awed by Victor's dedication and stamina. He pauses before we hang up. "You wouldn't happen to be the daughter," he says. "I know there is a daughter on record." The phrasing is delicate, his tone nonjudgmental. If I were the daughter I might very well own up.

| | |

Mid-morning I notice the Dog Lady handing Natalie bananas and other food. She stands close by for quite a while, keeping the dog reigned in just enough that he barely misses Natalie as he shoots his leash, time and time again. As soon as her visitors leave, Natalie is up and about, rifling through bags, finally making an empty-handed trip down the driveway to the basement-level garage. I want to think she was able to sleep back there, out of the wind, but the cart looks undisturbed, and I can't imagine she'd desert it all night. Maybe she has discovered a "private" toilet spot at last.

I see that I won't rest easy now till she's gone. My nerves are stretched out tight over the distance between us, suspended along this one very thin and anxiously wired connection. Despite all contrary efforts, I end up keeping a constant north window vigil. (A bumper sticker at the beach said "I ♥ Drapes.") I force myself to drive to the library and stay past dark.

| | DECEMBER 15

It looks like snow today, white skies and heavy air, barely out of the forties by noon. The worst rainstorm in years is predicted for tonight, with temperatures down into the thirties and heavy winds. The thought of Natalie soaking wet and shivering among her bags leaves me feeling queasy. I caught a brief but definite whiff of her in my hallway closet this morning, though nothing of hers is there except the skirt she never even tried on. Olfactory hallucinations. Maybe the flu is coming on. Or maybe I've caught some nasal madness from Lady Jane. I tell myself Natalie has been through so much that she can make it through one more rough night. I light a small white candle to honor the hope that she might be picked up tomorrow, though Victor made no such promise at all.

| | DECEMBER 16

When I get in from work, May and the Dog Lady are standing in animated conversation near Natalie's cart, which sits precariously balanced over the curb, one front wheel in the gutter. I go running up the hill to find out what the women know. It was May who saw the pickup.

"Four nice-looking men," she says. "I mean, they were just as nice looking as could be, and they knew what they were doing, the way they spoke with her and all. Four nice-looking gentlemen in a very large kind of van that said "Ambulance" or "Allied Medical" or something like that. Oh, but she gave them hell, don't think she didn't. You could hear her all over the neighborhood, and that's in spite of the wind. They were reasoning with her, and she was yelling her head off. For a while I didn't think she was going to go with them—she wanted to take *everything* with her, and they would only take a few bags. Oh, she put up quite a fuss about having to leave things on the sidewalk. Language I won't repeat, thank you very much. But then finally she did climb in and they closed the doors. I don't envy them a bit riding in a closed car with her, but that's exactly what they did. So that was that, and thank God it's over with."

All through this May has been holding onto her red felt hat to keep it from blowing away. She is holding her hat, and the Dog Lady is holding onto her dog's collar with one hand, a Kentucky Fried Chicken sack in the other. I hold onto the shopping cart.

"I brought her some food," the Dog Lady says, vaguely waving the sack and sounding almost disappointed. I am feeling so unburdened and exhilarated that I think she can't get on my nerves today, but she manages. "I fed her all the time," she says. "And I had some of the Sisters come out to see her every week. Some of the things she would say, though. She spoke so terrible about the priests and what they supposedly did to her. You can't imagine what she said about the priests. And she herself was supposed to be a healer and all this. I just hope no one thinks this woman is a Catholic, really, not after the things she says."

I search her face for some sign of awareness that she has just uttered something appalling, but the woman looks as if she's waiting to be congratulated. Outrage inspires outrageousness.

"Oh, she's Catholic, all right," I hear myself saying. "One of her paper bags was full of nothing but rosaries. Actually, she's the most devout Catholic I know. Actually, that was my favorite thing about her. She seemed to have a direct line to Mary. And such a spontaneously eucharistic attitude toward food, don't you think?"

Neither the Dog Lady nor May reveals the slightest indication she's heard this. "You know," May says, lowering her voice to a confidential tone, "there were certain of those bags that contained human waste. There is bound to be disease. Honestly, I've seen the woman squat right in the street. I had to look away, I really did."

"Goodness yes," the other woman chimes in. "And then she would try to tell me she was afraid she might catch something from Frederick here. She would absolutely *insist*. I thought that was almost cute, really, she was so funny about it."

Cold rain begins to blow in our faces, so I'm spared the need for a sudden excuse to leave. The three of us set off quickly in different directions, abandoning Natalie's cushions, seven or eight bags, and the cart itself, which is by no means empty but appears to have been relieved of everything substantial.

At the foot of my steps I meet Velma, who is also scurrying in from the rain. "What happened to your old woman?" she asks cheerily. "Did she die?"

"No, she just went to the hospital," I say.

"Oh, that's good, that's good," Velma says. "Glad to hear it. She never did belong on our street. Maybe they'll put her away somewhere."

The apartment feels dark and peculiarly empty. Whiskey sounds good, or some kind of cordial. I have an impulse to call everyone I know and tell them Natalie has been picked up, but then I don't really feel like talking. I make tea and lie flat on the floor and listen to Steely Dan.

> *They got a name for the winners in the world,*
> *And I want a name when I lose.*

They call Alabama the Crimson Tide,
Call me Deacon Blues.

I imagine Natalie shiny clean in a hospital gown, sitting up in bed, alert and alternately demanding or refusing something from the nurses. She will put them through their paces. I wonder if they had to throw all her stuff away or if it can be laundered for when she leaves. At least she'll be in on Christmas Day. Probably I could fry in hell for making up the thing about rosaries. With Natalie gone there is the sudden weight of watching out for myself.

| | |

In the days that followed, Natalie's remaining bags gradually disappeared from the sidewalk, while her cart ended up down the hill, parked at the curb, in fact, right in front of my apartment building. Perhaps that was accidental, or perhaps someone in the neighborhood wished to imply that this pile of trash (truly trash now, without Natalie to insist on its redefinition as property) belonged to me. For several days the cart sat curbside, first on one side of the street and then the other, its contents apparently undisturbed: a dingy foam rubber pillow, bereft of its case; a bright blue tin that once held Danish cookies; a child's pale pink sweater with rhinestones on the sleeves; a box of broken crayons; a bagful of dirty styrofoam cups and paper plates; and, sticking through a battered brown bag, a rusty metal garden tool, possibly one of Natalie's weapons. Visible from the side, among sundry other debris, was a crushed golden box, the box that once contained Natalie's new hat-and-glove set, the box that made them seem to her like "a gift of the Magi." I stubbornly refused to dispose of these things or even resituate the cart, which was interfering with parking space.

At last one day the whole shebang disappeared except for a few stray plates in the gutter. Protruding from beneath one of them lay a significant wad of Natalie's hair, all the dull, gray-blonde hair she had saved from her diligent combings, almost enough to comprise a standard, if badly matted, wig. The sight of it was chilling, oddly evocative of death and decay, but also a poignant embodiment of both Natalie's madness and her proud and sweet desire for sane routine. I couldn't bring myself to touch the hair, but neither could I leave it as it was. I managed to scoop it with one paper plate onto another and carry it back to Mrs. Moller's bin, but tossing it in loose didn't feel right, either, so I covered the hair with the other plate, brought them upstairs, and stapled them together, an arrangement I think Natalie might well have admired, even if I did waste a brand new plastic bag for disposal.

POSTSCRIPT

Natalie did not return to the streets following her three-week hospital stay. With treatment and medication she became stable enough to accept assistance from the Department of Mental Health. She was assigned a case manager who helped her obtain Supplemental Security Income, and she was placed in a licensed community care facility, where she still resided as of this writing.

A.N.

HOMELESSNESS: RESOURCES

FOR INFORMATION ABOUT homelessness and mental illness, including annotated bibliographies and research summaries, contact:

> National Resource Center on Homelessness
> and Severe Mental Illness
> 262 Delaware Avenue
> Delmar, NY 12054
> 800/444-7415

Locally, you may contact your Department of Mental Health, Mental Health Association, or Alliance for the Mentally Ill support groups. National Alliance for the Mentally Ill can be reached at 800/950-6264.

ABOUT THE AUTHOR

ANN NIETZKE has worked in a psychiatric shelter for people who are homeless and mentally ill since 1986. Her novel *Windowlight* (Capra Press, 1982; Picador, London, 1984) won the Los Angeles PEN Award for Best First Fiction. Her short stories have appeared in *Shenandoah, Other Voices,* and *The Massachusetts Review.* Nonfiction has appeared in *The Village Voice, Saturday Review, Cosmopolitan, CALYX Journal,* and elsewhere.

From 1974 until its demise in 1979, she was a contributing editor to *Human Behavior Magazine,* writing feature-length articles on media and communications. Several of these articles have been reprinted in textbook anthologies, including *Readings in Psychology and Human Experience, The Media Reader, Mass Media Issues, The Meaning of Sociology, Mass Media and Society, Society As It Is,* and *Strategies in Prose.*

Nietzke is a recipient of a Creative Writing Fellowship from the National Endowment for the Arts Literature Program and a MacDowell Colony Residency-in-writing.

She has a Master of Arts in English from Illinois State University. She is currently at work on a collection of short fiction.

Selected Titles from Award-Winning CALYX Books

Color Documentary by LuAnn Keener. Poetry that exquisitely investigates our relationships with the natural world—animals and their plight in the modern world—while exploring the dominant role of humans and our own endangerment.
ISBN 0-934971-39-0, $11.95, paper; ISBN 0-934971-40-4, $21.95, cloth.

Light in the Crevice Never Seen by Haunani-Kay Trask. The first book of poetry by an indigenous Hawaiian to be published in North America, *Light* is a native woman's impassioned and lyrical account of her land and people.
ISBN 0-934971-37-4, $11.95, paper; ISBN 0-934971-38-2, $21.95, cloth.

The Violet Shyness of Their Eyes: Notes from Nepal by Barbara J. Scot. A moving account of a western woman's transformative sojourn in Nepal as she reaches mid-life. PNBA Book Award.
ISBN 0-934971-35-8, $14.95, paper; ISBN 0-934971-36-6, $24.95, cloth.

Open Heart by Judith Mickel Sornberger. An elegant and moving collection of poetry rooted in a woman's relationships with family, ancestors, and the world.
ISBN 0-934971-31-5, $9.95, paper; ISBN 0-934971-32-3, $19.95, cloth.

Raising the Tents by Frances Payne Adler. A personal and political volume of poetry, documenting a woman's discovery of her voice. Finalist, WESTAF Book Award.
ISBN 0-934971-33-1, $9.95, paper; ISBN 0-934971-34-x, $19.95, cloth.

Killing Color by Charlotte Watson Sherman. These compelling, mythical short stories by a gifted storyteller delicately explore the African-American experience. Washington Governor's Award.
ISBN 0-934971-17-X, $9.95, paper; ISBN 0-934971-18-8, $19.95, cloth.

Mrs. Vargas and the Dead Naturalist by Kathleen Alcalá. Fourteen stories set in Mexico and the Southwestern U.S., written in the tradition of magical realism.
ISBN 0-934971-25-0, $9.95, paper; ISBN 0-934971-26-9, $19.95, cloth.

Black Candle by Chitra Divakaruni. Lyrical and honest poems that chronicle significant moments in the lives of South Asian women. Gerbode Award.
ISBN 0-934971-23-4, $9.95, paper; ISBN 0-934971-24-2, $19.95 cloth.

Ginseng and Other Tales from Manila by Marianne Villanueva. Poignant short stories set in the Philippines. Manila Critic's Circle National Literary Award Nominee.
ISBN 0-934971-19-6, $9.95, paper; ISBN 0-934971-20-X, $19.95, cloth.

COLOPHON

Text is set in Stone Serif, with headings in Caxton Light.
Typesetting and production prepared by
ImPrint Services, Corvallis, Oregon.